Another Taste of Florida

The Best of
"Thought You'd Never Ask"

Another Taste of Florida

The Best of
"Thought You'd Never Ask"

By Dorothy Chapman
Edited By Heather J. McPherson

Tribune Publishing
Orlando/1993

Copyright © 1993
Tribune Publishing
75 East Amelia Street, Orlando, Florida 32801

Written by Dorothy Chapman
Edited by Heather J. McPherson
Designed by Eileen Schechner
Cover photo by Jimm Roberts
Printed in the United States
July 1993

ISBN 0-941263-75-4

Tribune Publishing

Editorial Director: George C. Biggers III
Managing Editor: Dixie Kasper
Senior Editor: Kathleen M. Kiely
Production Manager: Ken Paskman
Editorial Designer: Bill Henderson
Editorial Designer: Joy Dickinson

Chapman, Dorothy, 1921-
    Another taste of Florida : the best of "Thought you'd never ask" /
by Dorothy Chapman ; edited by Heather J. McPherson.
        p.   cm.
    Includes index.
    ISBN 0-941263-75-4
    1. Cookery.   I. McPherson, Heather J.   II. Title.
TX714.C465   1993
641.5 — dc20   93-4843
                                                         CIP

About the author

Dorothy Chapman was the first staff food editor at *The Orlando Sentinel*. She was born in New York, grew up in Arizona and graduated from Arizona State University in Tempe. Before moving to Orlando in 1959, Chapman was a writer and radio commentator, an advertising manager for a large Western retail store and had her own advertising and public relations company.

In Central Florida, she worked briefly for a weekly newspaper, the now defunct *Corner Cupboard*. She began her career at The *Orlando Sentinel* as a society writer. Before she became the *Sentinel*'s food editor in 1971, Chapman had been women's editor, Lake County editor and fashion editor.

In her early days as food editor, Chapman was a one-woman show — writing stories and headlines, laying out pages and editing wire service copy. She has won awards for both writing and page design. She served as president of both the Central Florida Chapter of the Society of Professional Journalists and the Florida Press Club. She also served two terms on the Governor's Commission on the Status of Women.

Her "Thought You'd Never Ask" column, which has run for almost 20 years, provides readers with their favorite restaurant recipes. Chapman retired from the *Sentinel* in 1986 and continues to write her column for the Food section.

Retirement has meant a full roster of activities. Chapman is especially proud of her work with the March of Dimes and the organization's annual Gourmet Gala. She is on the Advisory Committee for the Orange County Home Extension Service and is president of her condominium association. Chapman has three daughters, Amy Elliot Lutz, Rosemary Chancellor and Deborah Claire Snyder. She has four grandchildren.

Acknowledgments

Many thanks to the following people who made this book possible:

Heather J. McPherson, food editor of *The Orlando Sentinel*, who pulled together the recipes in this book from the *Sentinel*'s library and supervised the book's production from start to finish.

Photographer Jimm Roberts, who shot the lovely color cover.

Tony Pace, executive chef for Davgar restaurants, and Alan Clapsadale, pastry chef for Davgar's Harvey's Bistro, for creating the decadent Chocolate-Raspberry Mousse featured on the cover. (You'll find the recipe on page 182.) Also, a nod to John Cicchetti, manager of Harvey's Bistro, for his cooperation.

Pier 1 Imports and *Sentinel* food writer Charlotte Balcomb Lane, for loaning the tableware for the cover photograph.

Tribune Publishing's Dixie Kasper, Bill Henderson, Ken Paskman and Eileen Schechner for their creative input and production support.

And most of all, the wonderful letter writers who fuel my weekly column in *The Orlando Sentinel*, and the talented Central Florida chefs who make their recipes available.

This ongoing interest in fine food and recognition of culinary talent shines a well-deserved spotlight on the Central Florida restaurant scene.

*To my four grandchildren
Christopher, Julie, Jenny and Dan —
the wonder of joy, laughter and love.*

Contents

Introduction

When "Thought You'd Never Ask" was launched in *The Orlando Sentinel*'s Food section years ago, it was planned as a forum for questions about nutrition.

We soon discovered people were more interested in the secrets of Florida restaurants. Seventeen years later I'm still peeking into chef's pots and rummaging through cookbooks to help readers create memorable meals at home. The letters have been gracious, warm and sometimes fodder for a chuckle. A writer in the early days wanted the recipe for Wonder Bread. Another person requested *every* recipe from the Nine Dragons menu at Epcot Center.

Then there was the woman who sent in a list of requests from 16 restaurants. Needless to say, I couldn't fulfill those requests in the column.

The most rewarding aspect of writing this column has been the enthusiastic response from Central Florida's talented chefs, independent restaurateurs and our magnificent resorts. The recipes in this collection have been tested in professional and home kitchens throughout the state. I hope you enjoy sharing them with your family and friends.

Dorothy Chapman

Appetizers

Lau Lau Clams is an impressive dish. Tourists who visited Walt Disney World in the '70s will remember it from the Papeete Bay Verandah's dinner buffet.

Polynesian Village Hotel's Lau Lau Clams
Walt Disney World, Lake Buena Vista

10 fresh clams
1½ pounds frozen chopped
 spinach
½ cup chopped bacon
1 cup chopped cabbage
1 tablespoon ground fresh
 ginger
⅛ cup oyster sauce
1 tablespoon fish base
⅛ cup sesame seed oil
4 drops Tabasco sauce
Bechamel Sauce (recipe
 follows)
Mornay Sauce (recipe follows)
Grated Parmesan cheese

Wash clams under cold water until no more sand is present. (Make sure that clams stay firmly closed; this indicates clams are fresh and alive. Discard any that don't close firmly.)

Bring ½ quart of water to a boil; add clams. When clams open to about ½ inch remove them from the water. Cool clams and then pull apart. Take meat out, chop and reserve for spinach mixture. Reserve clam shells. To make spinach mixture, saute bacon until browned. Remove bacon. Saute cabbage in the bacon drippings. When cabbage is half cooked, add drained spinach, folding it into the cabbage. Add chopped clams, drained bacon, ginger, oyster sauce, fish base, sesame seed oil and Tabasco sauce. Finish cooking until cabbage is transparent. Drain any excessive moisture.

Fold half of the Bechamel Sauce into mixture; let cool. Stuff reserved shells about three-quarters full. Ladle Mornay Sauce over stuffing. Top with Parmesan. Broil until sauce turns a light brown. Serve at once. The clam shells can be stuffed ahead of time with the spinach mixture and refrigerated or frozen.

Makes 10 servings.

Bechamel Sauce

¼ cup plus 1 tablespoon
    butter or margarine
¼ cup minced onions
½ cup flour
2 cups milk
½ teaspoon salt or to taste
White pepper to taste
Nutmeg to taste
1 bay leaf

In a saucepan, melt butter or margarine. Add minced onions and saute for about 3 minutes. Add flour and cook for about 1 minute more. Remove pan from heat. Heat milk to a slight simmer. Add salt, white pepper, nutmeg and bay leaf. Let simmer for about 2 minutes, then add flour mixture and cook for about 5 minutes until thick. Reserve half of the mixture to make Mornay Sauce. Use remaining half in recipe as directed.

Mornay Sauce

Reserved Bechamel Sauce
½ cup milk
2 egg yolks
½ cup grated Parmesan cheese

In a saucepan over medium-low heat, combine milk and reserved Bechamel Sauce. Stir mixture until it thickens. Add egg yolks and grated Parmesan cheese. Stir and use as directed in recipe.

The Lakeside Inn's beautiful Beauclaire dining room is the perfect setting for a special occasion meal.

Lakeside Inn's Stuffed Mushrooms
Mount Dora

20 to 25 large mushroom caps
2 cups crab meat
2 cups bread crumbs
$^{1}/_{2}$ cup mayonnaise
2 eggs, beaten
$^{1}/_{2}$ cup chopped celery
$^{1}/_{2}$ cup cream cheese, softened
  to room temperature
$^{1}/_{4}$ cup chopped onions
$^{1}/_{4}$ cup chopped green pepper
1 teaspoon ground oregano
1 tablespoon curry powder

Sauce:
1 cup mayonnaise
4 eggs, beaten
2 tablespoons stone-ground
  mustard
1 teaspoon Lawry's Seasoned
  Salt

Mix together crab meat, bread crumbs, $^{1}/_{2}$ cup mayonnaise, 2 beaten eggs, chopped celery, softened cream cheese, chopped onions, chopped green pepper, ground oregano and curry powder.

Stuff mushroom caps with mixture.

Place in a lightly greased baking pan. Mix together 1 cup mayonnaise, 4 beaten eggs, 2 tablespoons mustard, Lawry's Seasoned Salt. Spoon mixture over mushrooms. Bake for 15 minutes in a 350F oven.

Makes 5 to 6 appetizer servings.

The key to this Florida favorite is properly tenderizing the meat. Alligator meat is available at stores that specialize in fish and shellfish.

Gary's Duck Inn's Gator Tail and Swamp Sauce
Orlando

2 pounds alligator tail meat
2 eggs beaten with 2 cups milk
   for wash
Self-rising flour seasoned to
   taste with pepper, salt and
   granulated garlic
Peanut oil for deep-frying

Marinade:
2 cups salad oil
¾ cup red-wine vinegar
1 teaspoon garlic powder
½ teaspoon black pepper
1 teaspoon oregano
Dash of salt

Swamp sauce:
1 cup mayonnaise
⅛ cup yellow mustard
⅛ cup horseradish
Dash of Worcestershire sauce
Dash of Tabasco sauce
Juice of 1 lemon

Remove all fat and sinew from gator meat before preparing. Tenderize in cubing machine or place between sheets of wax paper and pound with a mallet to about ½-inch thickness. Cut across grain for more tender pieces into 1-inch squares.

Combine all ingredients listed for marinade.

Let gator marinate in salad oil mixture in the refrigerator for 24 hours.

At preparation time, remove meat from marinade, dip in egg wash then dredge in seasoned flour.

Heat peanut oil in deep-fryer to 350F. Deep-fry meat pieces carefully about 1 minute. Remove with slotted spoon and drain on paper towels.

Stir together swamp sauce ingredients.

Serve deep fried gator tail with Swamp Sauce on the side for dipping.

Makes 4 servings.

At Marrakesh, Walt Disney World guests can sample the wonderful, exotic cuisine of Morocco. This eggplant salad can be served hot or chilled.

Restaurant Marrakesh's Zaalouk
Epcot's Moroccan Showcase, Lake Buena Vista

4 eggplants cut in 2-inch
  squares
1/4 cup olive oil
1 medium-size tomato, cubed
1 tablespoon minced fresh
  garlic
1/4 cup red-wine vinegar
1 tablespoon tomato paste
1/8 teaspoon crushed red
  pepper
1/8 cup lemon juice
1 tablespoon paprika
1/2 teaspoon cumin

Boil eggplant until very soft in 2 quarts salted water. Drain well and set aside. In a heavy skillet heat olive oil. Add tomato, saute until not quite soft, stir in eggplant.

In a small mixing bowl, combine remaining ingredients. Mix until smooth, add mixture to eggplant and tomato. Cook on medium heat, stirring frequently, for 10 minutes, then on low heat for 30 minutes.

Serve hot or chilled.

Makes 4 servings.

Recipe notes: This recipe can yield up to 8 servings depending on the size of eggplants used.

Here's a another goodie from Marrakesh. This fancy-sounding appetizer is simply a lightly seasoned tomato and green pepper salad.

Restaurant Marrakesh's Choukchouka
Epcot's Moroccan Showcase, Lake Buena Vista

3 green bell peppers, cubed
6 medium-size tomatoes, cubed
¼ cup olive oil
½ tablespoon minced fresh garlic
1 tablespoon tomato paste
1 tablespoon paprika
½ tablespoon cumin
½ tablespoon white pepper
½ tablespoon salt

In large skillet, heat olive oil.
Saute peppers and minced garlic together until peppers are soft. Add tomatoes and balance of ingredients. Saute until tender, about 15 minutes.
Serve hot or chilled.
Makes 4 servings.

Central Florida caterers Jon and Kathleen Berry serve this enticing dip with Melba toast or wheat crackers.

Celebrations Unlimited's Artichoke Dip
Winter Park

1 (14-ounce) can artichoke hearts (not marinated)
1 cup low-calorie mayonnaise
1 package dry Good Seasons Italian Dressing mix
1 cup grated Parmesan cheese
1 teaspoon or to taste Dijon mustard

Drain artichoke hearts and squeeze until excess liquid is removed. Put in the work bowl of a food processor and, using the on-off switch or pulse button, chop into small, coarse pieces. Be careful not to puree the artichokes.

Put chopped artichokes into a mixing bowl and blend in the remaining ingredients.

Spoon artichoke mixture into a microwave safe serving dish, cover and vent with plastic wrap. Microwave on high (100 percent) power for 2 to 3 minutes, stirring often.

The mixture should not be overcooked, just heated through and blended.

Serve immediately with Melba toast or crackers of choice.

Makes 10 servings.

Fred and Margaret Fenwick have been catering Central Florida functions for years. This hot crab dip is one of their most popular menu items.

Fenwick Catering's Hot Crab Meat Dip
Orlando

1 pound Alaskan crab meat, coarsely chopped
1 pound cream cheese
1/2 cup mayonnaise
1 bunch green onions, top and bulbs finely chopped
2 dashes Tabasco sauce
1 teaspoon Lea & Perrins Worcestershire sauce
1/2 cup slivered almonds, toasted

Preheat oven to 350F.
Blend together all ingredients except nuts. Spoon into bake-and-serve dish. Sprinkle top with slivered almonds. Place in preheated oven and bake 20 minutes. Serve warm with crackers, Melba rounds, or toast points.

Served over any pasta, this appetizer could easily be used as an entree. Chef-owner Gus Stamatin always adds a special flair to his food.

Gus' Villa Rosa's Mussels Marinara
Orlando

1 (15-ounce) can tomatoes, crushed
2 cloves garlic, finely chopped
1 tablespoon chopped parsley
1 jalapeno pepper, seeded and finely chopped
1 tablespoon finely chopped onion
2 tablespoons olive oil
1 teaspoon oregano
½ teaspoon salt
1 teaspoon sugar
24 mussels, steamed on the half shell
Mozzarella or provolone cheese, coarsely grated
Vermicelli, spaghetti or linguini

Saute tomatoes, garlic, parsley, jalapeno pepper and onion in olive oil. Add seasonings and simmer for 15 minutes.

Arrange mussels in the half shell in a baking pan. Cover mussels with sauce and refrigerate for 1 hour. Spoon cheese over mussels.

Heat oven to 350F. Bake mussels for 10 minutes.

Serve immediately with pasta of choice.

Makes 6 servings.

This is an elegant appetizer presentation for a festive party buffet. It can be made ahead of time and chilled until serving time. It was created by the talented chefs at Edible's Etcetera.

Edibles' Crab & Avocado Stuffed Potatoes
Altamonte Springs

12 new potatoes
Salt and pepper to taste
2 pounds Alaskan crab meat
1 large avocado, diced
2 teaspoons lemon juice
¼ cup chopped green onions
1 tablespoon chopped fresh
   dill
1 tablespoon shredded
   carrots
Dill sprigs for garnish
Finely diced carrot for
   garnish

Chantilly cream:
½ cup mayonnaise
½ cup whipped heavy
   cream
Dash nutmeg
Salt and pepper to taste

Boil or microwave the potatoes until just soft when pierced with a fork. Cut cooked potatoes in half. Cut a slender slice from the round bottom so that the potato will sit upright. Hollow center of potato with a melon ball scoop or a small spoon (reserve scooped out potato for another use). Season potato boats with salt and pepper.

Combine mayonnaise, whipping cream, nutmeg and salt and pepper to make Chantilly cream; set aside.

Drain crab meat on paper towels. Cut avocado into small pieces and soak in lemon juice for 1 minute to prevent browning. In a medium-size bowl, combine crab meat, avocado, scallions, dill, carrots and salt and pepper. Add Chantilly cream and stir just to coat ingredients.

Stuff avocado-crab mixture into potato halves. Garnish with finely diced carrots and a fresh dill sprig. Chill until serving time.

Makes 24 servings.

Shao mai are morsels of seasoned pork steamed in egg roll skins. To prepare this, you will need a bamboo steamer or a steamer insert for a large pot or wok.

Jimmy & Mimi's Tea Garden's Shao Mai
Fern Park

1 pound thin egg roll skins
1 pound minced or ground
  pork
1 cup minced water chestnuts
1/2 cup finely chopped green
  onions
1/2 teaspoon salt
1/4 teaspoon pepper
1 tablespoon sugar
1 tablespoon soy sauce
1 tablespoon sesame oil
1 tablespoon white wine
Sauce:
5 tablespoons sesame oil
5 tablespoons oyster sauce
1/4 cup chopped scallions

Stack egg roll skins and cut into quarters. Trim off corners to make rounds; set aside. Mix pork, water chestnuts, onions, salt, pepper, sugar, soy sauce, sesame oil and white wine.

Put 1 teaspoon of filling in center of each quartered egg roll round, pleat edges together, folding over filling slightly (like flower petals). Leave the center of filling uncovered. Place as many dumplings as will fit without touching in a 2-inch deep pan. Add 1 cup boiling water. Place pan on a steamer rack. Pour boiling water into a large wok or the pot that will hold the steamer. The rack should be about 2 inches above water level. Cover and steam for about 20 minutes. You may need to add additional water to keep water level high and on a full boil.

To make the sauce, mix sesame oil, oyster sauce and scallions.

At end of steaming, remove pan from heat and let cool until the cover can be removed. Put dumplings on a platter. Do not spoon sauce over dumplings until ready to eat.

Makes 53 to 55 small dumplings or 9 appetizer servings.

The heart-of-the-city location is a popular lunch and dinner stop for the downtown crowd.

Lee's Lakeside's Stuffed Mushrooms
Orlando

1 pound artificial crab legs, chopped
2 (6-ounce) cans crab meat, drained
2 eggs
2 teaspoons lemon pepper
2 teaspoons chopped chives
2 teaspoons seafood seasoning
$1/3$ teaspoon garlic powder
$1/2$ cup cracker meal
3 cups bread crumbs
$1/2$ cup mayonnaise (do not use salad dressing)
1 tablespoon melted butter
$1/4$ cup finely chopped celery
$1/4$ cup finely chopped onion
$1/2$ teaspoon Accent
$2^1/2$ to 3 dozen jumbo mushroom caps
Melted butter

In large bowl, mix together all ingredients except mushroom caps and last listing of melted butter.

Place mushroom caps on baking sheets, mound each with crab meat stuffing, drizzle with melted butter.

Bake in a 350F oven for 12 to 15 minutes or until stuffing is golden and mushrooms firm but tender. Serve immediately.

Makes $2^1/2$ to 3 dozen caps or 9 servings.

13

The chef takes a creative approach to this traditional appetizer and prepares it with whole shrimp instead of the usual mashed and seasoned shrimp mixture.

China Garden's Shrimp Toast
Winter Park

4 large shrimp
Salt and pepper to taste
Flour or cornstarch for
   dredging
2 eggs beaten
2 slices white bread
Sesame seeds or bread crumbs
   for garnish
Vegetable oil for frying

Shell and clean shrimp with salted water, cut to butterfly and season to taste with salt and pepper. Dip in flour or cornstarch, then into beaten eggs. Trim crust from bread slices, cut each slice in half into triangles.

Top each piece of bread with a prepared shrimp, place firmly so flour-egg mixture will make shrimp adhere to bread.

Heat oil to 325F, deep-fry shrimp toast until well browned.

Garnish with sesame seeds or bread crumbs.

Serve immediately.

Makes 1 serving.

Here's another variation on the stuffed mushroom cap theme. This recipe uses chopped fresh spinach to add color and flavor to the stuffing mixture.

Anthony's Stuffed Mushroom Caps
Winter Park

2 pounds fresh spinach
1 cup bread crumbs
2 tablespoons chopped onion
1 teaspoon chopped garlic
1 cup grated fresh Parmesan
   cheese
1 cup mayonnaise
2 egg yolks
12 large fancy mushrooms
6 ounces snow crab meat,
   cleaned and picked apart

Cook spinach, drain well and chop.

Place in a mixing bowl, stir in bread crumbs, onion, garlic, cheese and mayonnaise. Blend egg yolks, fold into spinach mixture.

Clean and remove stems from mushrooms. Fill caps with stuffing and top with crab meat.

Bake in 350F oven until golden brown, about 20 minutes.

Makes 2 servings of 6 caps each; recipe doubles easily for 4 servings.

At this picturesque Orange County restaurant, an appetizer serving of this dish includes 10 pickle slices on a bed of lettuce and horseradish sauce.

Townsend's Plantation's Deep-Fried Pickles
Apopka

Kosher dill pickles
Golden Dipt all-purpose
  batter mix
Vegetable oil for frying
Horseradish sauce of choice

Slice desired number of kosher dill pickles into six to eight slices per pickle. Dip slices in Golden Dipt all-purpose batter prepared according to package directions. (Golden Dipt brand batter mix is available in most supermarkets.) Deep-fry pickles in vegetable oil heated to 350F until golden brown.

Serve as an appetizer with horseradish sauce.

There are many variations for bruschetta, but most recipes include garlic, olive oil and tomatoes. La Romantica is no longer open but in its heyday this was a favorite on the appetizer menu.

La Romantica's Bruschetta
Winter Park

1 pint cherry tomatoes
1 cup olive oil
3 tablespoons chopped fresh
   garlic
3 teaspoons salt
3 teaspoons white pepper
3 tablespoons dried oregano
3 tablespoons dried basil
Pinch of dried red pepper
Garlic powder to taste
Grated Parmesan cheese for
   garnish
Chopped fresh parsley for
   garnish
1 loaf Italian bread

Slice tomatoes into quarters.

Mix together all ingredients except bread for 1 to $1^1/2$ minutes. Let stand in refrigerator at least 3 hours.

To make slicing easier, put Italian bread in freezer for a short time. Cut bread into desired number of slices (about $^1/2$-inch thick).

Thoroughly mix again garlic and oil mixture.

Using a large spoon, ladle liquid (try to get 6 tomato quarters in each spoonful) on bread slices. Place bread slices on a baking sheet and put under broiler for two to three minutes or until slices are browned. Sprinkle slices with Parmesan cheese and parsley.

Serve immediately.

Makes about 15 to 25 slices.

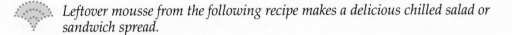

Leftover mousse from the following recipe makes a delicious chilled salad or sandwich spread.

Royal Orleans' Blackened Chicken Mousse
Orlando

Herb-Buttered French Bread (recipe follows)
6 (8-ounce) chicken breasts, skinned and boned
1 pint whipping cream
½ pound sour cream
½ cup trinity (a combination of equal amounts of ground green pepper, celery and onion)
1 teaspoon granulated garlic
Salt and cayenne pepper to taste

To blacken chicken, pound chicken into thin cutlets and marinate 30 minutes in a small portion of the Herb Butter mixture. In cast-iron skillet that is extremely hot, sear breasts on each side for $1^1/2$ minutes.

To make mousse, finely grind chicken and trinity vegetables. Whip cream; set aside.

Add all other ingredients to mousse, then fold in cream. Using a pastry bag, pipe rosettes of mousse into small serving dishes. Cover and refrigerate until serving time. (Other cuts of boneless chicken as well as cooked shrimp or crawfish may also be used in this recipe.)

Serve with Herb-Buttered French Bread (recipe follows on page 19).

Makes 36 appetizer servings.

Serve this crusty bread with any pasta dish or with Royal Orleans' Blackened Chicken Mousse.

Royal Orleans' Herb-Buttered French Bread
Orlando

French bread
1 pound butter, clarified
  (instructions follow)
2 teaspoons oregano
2 teaspoons basil
2 teaspoons thyme
2 teaspoons minced garlic
1 tablespoon Lea & Perrins
  Worcestershire sauce
1 teaspoon Tabasco sauce
½ cup dry vermouth
Salt and cayenne pepper to
  taste
Chopped parsley, paprika and
  grated Parmesan cheese for
  garnish

To clarify butter, cut into small pieces and melt over moderate heat. Skim off foam with spoon, remove pan from heat and let stand a few minutes to settle. Skim the clear yellow liquid off the milky residue and reserve; discard the residue in pan.

Mix clarified butter with other ingredients to make herb spread. Slice desired amount of French bread at an angle. Brush slices with herb butter and sprinkle with paprika, parsley and Parmesan cheese. Brown lightly under broiler and arrange attractively on plate with mousse. Herb butter freezes well.

This is one of the many fine Northern Italian specialties prepared by the chef of this intimate family-operated restaurant.

Palma Maria's Eggplant Rollatini
Casselberry

1 large eggplant
1½ pounds ricotta cheese
¼ cup grated Parmesan
    cheese
¾ cup shredded mozzarella
    cheese
2 egg yolks
1 teaspoon salt
¼ teaspoon pepper
¼ cup freshly chopped
    parsley
Marinara Sauce (recipe
    follows)
Sliced mozzarella (optional)

Peel eggplant if desired, slice into ½-inch thickness. Lightly salt on both sides; place in colander to drain.

To make filling, mix together ricotta, Parmesan, mozzarella, egg yolks, salt, pepper and parsley.

Rinse and pat dry eggplant slices. Put about two tablespoons of filling on each slice, roll and place seam-side down on buttered baking dish.

Top with Marinara Sauce or favorite tomato sauce and bake in 400F oven about 20 minutes or until tender. If desired, put slice of mozzarella on each roll and return to oven until cheese is melted.

Serve with Italian sausage or meatballs.

Makes 6 to 8 servings.

Marinara Sauce

1 small onion, chopped
2 cloves garlic, diced
$\frac{1}{4}$ cup olive oil
1 (1-pound) can plum tomatoes
Salt and pepper to taste
$\frac{1}{4}$ cup dry white wine
Chopped fresh parsley to taste
$\frac{1}{2}$ teaspoon chopped fresh
  basil
$\frac{1}{4}$ cup Parmesan cheese

Saute onion and garlic in olive oil until transparent. Add tomatoes crushed in juice, salt and pepper. Bring to boil, add white wine, parsley and basil.

Reduce heat and simmer about 30 minutes or until liquid is cooked down. Shortly before sauce is finished, stir in Parmesan cheese. Adjust seasonings.

Anna Marie's friendly staff and fine food make for an enjoyable evening out. The following is the restaurant's interpretation of oysters Rockefeller.

Anna Marie's Oysters Francoise
Melbourne

8 slices diced bacon
¼ cup chopped celery
¼ cup diced onion
1 teaspoon diced garlic
½ cup chopped green onion
1 cup cooked spinach, well
 drained
½ teaspoon salt
¼ teaspoon white pepper
⅛ teaspoon cayenne pepper
4 tablespoons white wine
3 tablespoons lemon juice
Bread crumbs (as needed)
24 fresh oysters
8 strips bacon, cooked
Remoulade sauce (bottled or
 your favorite recipe)

In a large skillet, saute bacon, celery, onion, garlic and green onion. Add spinach, salt, peppers, wine and lemon juice. Adjust seasonings to taste. Add bread crumbs as needed to absorb excess liquid.

Butter 4 individual casserole dishes. Fill dishes with spinach mixture; cover with oysters, about 6 per dish (depending on size).

Put 2 strips of bacon over each prepared casserole. Cover center of bacon with 3 tablespoons of remoulade sauce.

Bake casseroles at 400F for 10 minutes or until bubbly.

Makes 4 servings.

Orlando has a fabulous Peabody Hotel on International Drive. However, this recipe was requested from the chain's flagship operation in Memphis, Tenn.

Peabody's Poached Pineapples and Bananas
Memphis, Tenn.

½ gallon white wine
1½ cups sugar
½ cup vanilla extract
2 large pineapples, peeled, cored and cubed
10 bananas, peeled and sliced
2 cups heavy whipping cream
2 ounces Myers's dark rum
½ cup sugar
Pinch cinnamon

Over medium heat combine wine, sugar and vanilla. Add pineapple and poach until al dente (tender but lightly crisp). Pour liquid and pineapple mixture over bananas. Cool until mixture thickens. Beat heavy cream until it forms peaks. Fold in rum, then sugar. Top poached pineapple and bananas with whipped cream and sprinkle with cinnamon.

Makes 8 servings.

The secret to these crisp appetizer sticks is the milk bath. It's similar to the milk-soak method used in making onion rings.

Alfredo's Zucchine Fritti All' Alfredo
Epcot's Italian Showcase, Lake Buena Vista

2 pounds zucchini
2 cups milk
1 teaspoon salt
1⅛ cups flour
1⅛ cups bread crumbs
4 cups vegetable oil

Cut trimmed and washed zucchini into 3-inch strips. Add salt to milk. Soak cut zucchini in milk for 1 hour. If needed, add more milk to cover zucchini. Combine flour and bread crumbs. Remove zucchini from milk bath and dredge well in flour-crumb mixture. Allow zucchini to rest for 30 minutes.

Heat vegetable oil to 325F and fry zucchini until golden brown. Remove with a slotted spoon. Drain on paper towels and serve hot.

Makes 6 servings.

The Columbia is Florida's premiere Spanish restaurant chain. The family-owned business was founded in 1905 in Tampa's Ybor City.

Columbia Restaurant's Ceviche
Ybor City, Sarasota, St. Petersburg, St. Augustine

2 pounds fresh grouper fillet
1 medium onion
½ medium green pepper
¼ sweet Cuban pepper
   (optional)
2 tablespoons chopped fresh
   cilantro leaves
¼ cup white wine
¼ cup olive oil
Salt and pepper to taste
Oregano to taste
10 whole lemons, juiced
Fresh fruit for garnish
Parsley for garnish
Black olives for garnish

Cut boneless, skinless fillet into julienne strips or small chunks. Cut onion, sweet and green pepper, in very fine julienne pieces, and chop cilantro finely. In a non-metal bowl, toss vegetables with sliced grouper, wine and olive oil. Season with salt, pepper, and oregano.

Cover completely with lemon juice and refrigerate for at least 10 hours. Using a slotted spoon, serve very cold on bed of lettuce and garnish with fresh fruit and melon slices. Sprinkle with black olives and parsley.

Makes 8 appetizer servings.

Recipe note: The lemon juice "cooks" the fish.

Deep-fried chicken wings are a hit at any gathering. These are soaked in an intriguing Oriental marinade before frying.

Kona Village's Chicken Wings
Altamonte Springs

2½ pounds chicken wings, either entire wings or drummettes
1 teaspoon salt
½ teaspoon sugar
½ teaspoon white pepper
¼ teaspoon sesame oil
1 egg, beaten
1 tablespoon white wine
½ teaspoon five-spice powder (available in the Asian foods section of most supermarkets)
1 teaspoon garlic powder
2 to 3 drops yellow food color
½ teaspoon monosodium glutamate (optional)
4 tablespoons all-purpose flour
2 tablespoons cornstarch
Vegetable oil for frying

Dry chicken wings well. Let meat stand long enough so that skin is dry enough to allow marinade to cling.

Mix together balance of ingredients except flour and cornstarch.

In a separate bowl or on wax paper, mix flour and cornstarch. If more breading is desired, add more flour and cornstarch in the same proportion.

Dip chicken wings in marinade to coat well, dredge in flour mixture. If a thin crust is desired, dredge lightly, if a crisper texture is preferred, use more of the flour mixture. Arrange wings in a pan and refrigerate overnight.

Heat vegetable oil to 350F. Deep-fry chicken for about 10 minutes or until wings float to top.

Makes 4 appetizer servings.

Here's a smooth French bistro pate to spread on toast points with chopped onions and peppers.

Le Coq au Vin's Warm Chicken Liver Pate
Orlando

1 pound fresh chicken livers
½ cup milk
4 tablespoons diced onions
1 small clove garlic, diced
2 eggs
Salt and pepper to taste
2 tablespoons port wine
   (optional)
5 ounces rendered chicken fat
4 tablespoons whipping cream

Clean livers by cutting off all pieces of membrane or fat; soak in milk for 30 minutes, drain.

Place liver, onions and garlic in blender container and blend at medium speed. When well blended, reduce speed to low and add eggs one at a time, rendered cold chicken fat, whipping cream, wine, salt and pepper. When well blended, refrigerate for 30 minutes. Pour pate mixture into 5-ounce aluminum cups.

Place in shallow baking pan filled halfway with water and bake in 350F oven for 40 minutes.

Serve warm or cold with toast points, chopped onions, capers, stewed tomatoes or pickles.

Makes 4 servings.

Recipe notes: To render chicken fat, chop the fat into small pieces, add a little water and simmer in covered saucepan about 15 minutes. Remove from heat. When cold, lift out the congealed fat and refrigerate until ready to use.

The following recipe comes from one of Central Florida's most innovative caterers. From small gatherings to large parties, Edibles Etcetera makes any occasion special.

Edibles' Miniature Beef Kebabs
Altamonte Springs

2 pounds sirloin
$1/4$ cup salad oil
2 tablespoons cider vinegar
1 teaspoon minced onion
1 teaspoon minced garlic
$1/2$ teaspoon salt
1 teaspoon oregano
$1/2$ teaspoon pepper
1 tablespoon Dijon mustard
1 small bay leaf
2 large green peppers, cut into
　1-inch squares
1 large onion, cut into 1-inch
　squares
Cherry tomato halves
24 (6-inch) bamboo skewers

Cut sirloin into $1/2$-inch cubes; set aside.

In a saucepan, combine salad oil, cider vinegar, minced onion, garlic, salt, oregano, pepper, mustard and bay leaf. Heat to boiling, then remove from heat to cool.

Pour cooled mixture into a marinating container or glass bowl. Add green pepper and sirloin to oil and vinegar mixture. Cover and refrigerate overnight.

Preheat oven broiler.

Alternate meat, green pepper, onion squares and tomato halves on bamboo skewers.

Broil kebabs for 2 or 3 minutes, turn skewer and broil for 2 minutes more, or until meat is done.

Makes about 24 appetizers.

The following appetizer is from one of downtown Orlando's most innovative restaurants.

Lombardi's Calamari Fritti
Orlando

1 pound calamari, cut in small strips
Chopped parsley and lemon wedges for garnish
Oil for deep-frying

Sauce:
2 medium-size tomatotes, peeled and seeded
1 onion, coarsely chopped
1 clove garlic
4 ounces pepperocini (Italian peppers), stems removed
1 ounce fresh basil
1 bunch fresh parsley, stems removed
1 tablespoon drained capers
1 tablespoon tomato paste
1 teaspoon salt
1 teaspoon black pepper
1 teaspoon paprika
1½ cups red-wine vinegar
1 cup olive oil

Batter:
2 eggs
1 cup milk

Seasoned flour:
1 cup all-purpose flour
1 teaspoon kosher salt
1 teaspoon white pepper
1 teaspoon cayenne pepper

In a food processor, puree all ingredients listed for sauce. Set mixture aside.

Mix batter ingredients until well-blended and set aside.

Combine all ingredients for seasoned flour. Mix well with a fork.

Put calamari in batter and allow the excess to drip off. Dredge calamari in seasoned flour mixture.

Deep-fry in oil for 4 to 5 minutes.

Serve on top of sauce and garnish with lemon wedges and chopped parsley.

Makes 6 servings.

Soups

This delightfully rich lobster bisque recipe was developed by chef Harlan Goldstein. The elegant restaurant offers a splendid bird's-eye view of the Walt Disney World Marketplace.

Arthur's 27 Chef Harlan's Lobster Bisque
Buena Vista Palace, Lake Buena Vista

3 whole lobsters
1 tablespoon olive oil
4 ribs celery, chopped
3 carrots, chopped
2 medium onions, chopped
3 tomatoes, chopped
1 bay leaf
2 cloves garlic, minced
Salt to taste
Pepper to taste
Cayenne pepper to taste
1 cup Pernod liqueur
1 cup brandy
1 cup white wine
2 quarts fish stock
1 quart heavy cream

Remove tail and claw from lobsters. Add olive oil to large saucepan or stockpot. Over high heat, saute quickly until meat is tender. Remove and set aside.

To pot, add remaining lobster meat, chopped vegetables, bay leaf and seasonings to taste. Stir in Pernod, brandy and white wine and over high heat reduce volume by half. Lower heat, stir in fish stock and cream to thicken.

Simmer mixture for 30 minutes and strain. Remove meat from reserved tails and claws and use as garnish for soup.

Makes 10 servings.

This cafe was a popular dining spot in Orlando years ago. It was famous for its simple, uncomplicated fare and homey atmosphere.

The Bistro's Macaroni and Cheese Soup
Orlando

3 to 4 ribs celery, diced
1 large onion, chopped
1 clove garlic, crushed
½ stick butter
6 cups good chicken stock
½ tablespoon Worcestershire sauce
1 teaspoon crushed oregano leaves
8 ounces small sea shell macaroni
10 slices natural Wisconsin Cheddar cheese

Saute vegetables in butter until transparent. Add chicken stock and seasonings, stir. Over medium high heat, bring stock to serving temperature.

In another saucepan, cook macaroni following package directions. Drain and stir into hot stock. Ladle into bowls, top each serving with a cheese slice. The heat of the soup will melt the cheese.

Makes about 10 servings.

This popular Volusia County eatery has a spectacular view of the Indian River. Diners come daily by boat or car.

Riverview Charlie's Broccoli-Cauliflower Soup
New Smyrna Beach

1 bunch broccoli
1 head cauliflower
1 quart strong chicken stock
1 small onion, finely diced
2 quarts milk
1 cup chopped fresh parsley
1 tablespoon chopped fresh
   dill or 1 teaspoon dried dill
White pepper and salt to taste
1$\frac{1}{3}$ sticks butter, margarine
   or butter substitute
$\frac{1}{2}$ cup flour

Wash and trim broccoli and cauliflower. Remove florets, set aside. Mince stalks.

In a stockpot or kettle, heat water to a boil. Add stalks and simmer until tender; drain.

Puree cooked broccoli and cauliflower in the work bowl of a food processor or blender (follow manufacturer's directions for container capacity). Return mixture to stockpot.

Add onion, broccoli and cauliflower florets, milk, dill, parsley, salt and white pepper. Simmer mixture over medium heat (do not boil) until florets are tender but retain texture and color.

In a separate pan, melt butter or margarine, stir in flour to make a smooth roux. Stir into hot soup, reduce heat to low to prevent scorching and continue stirring until soup is thickened and smooth.

Adjust seasoning and, if needed, thin with additional milk to desired consistency.

Makes 14 large servings.

Sbarro's specializes in Southern Italian specialties. Serve this delicious soup with a light salad of mixed greens and warm Italian bread.

Sbarro's Leek and Roasted Garlic Soup
Winter Park

2 whole heads jumbo or extra-large garlic, unpeeled
Olive oil for brushing
½ cup olive oil
4 cups chopped leeks, bulb only (reserve some of the green tops for garnish)
1 cup finely chopped yellow onions
½ teaspoon white pepper
Salt to taste
6 cups fresh chicken stock or canned clear chicken broth
½ stick butter
5 tablespoons flour
2 cups heavy whipping cream

Preheat oven to 350F.

Put whole unpeeled heads of garlic on baking sheet, brush lightly with olive oil. Roast in preheated oven 25 minutes or until garlic is very soft. Allow heads to cool; cut off top of garlic heads, separate each clove and peel.

Finely chop garlic heads and set aside. Roasted garlic loses its assertiveness and is very sweet.

Add olive oil to heavy-bottomed kettle or stockpot.

Saute chopped onions and leeks for about 2 minutes or until translucent, do not brown. Stir in chopped roasted garlic, white pepper, salt and chicken stock. Bring mixture to a boil.

In a separate saucepan, melt butter and slowly stir in flour to make a roux. When well blended, stir slowly into soup stock, reduce heat and simmer 15 minutes, stirring occasionally.

Before serving, stir in heavy cream and remove from heat.

Garnish with chopped green tops of leeks.

Makes 8 servings.

Three Cheese and Onion Soup has been a consistent favorite among Universal Studio guests.

Universal's Three Cheese and Onion Soup
Universal Studios, Orlando

1³/₄ pounds (about 2¹/₂ large) peeled white onions, thinly sliced
2 tablespoons vegetable oil
2 teaspoons sherry
7 cups beef broth
2 cups chicken broth
1¹/₂ cups rice flour
1 cup warm water
1¹/₄ cups grated Swiss cheese
2 cups shredded mozzarella cheese
3 ounces brie, skin trimmed, diced
Salt and white pepper to taste
Cayenne pepper to taste
1 cup heavy cream

Over low heat, saute onions in vegetable oil until transparent; do not brown. Add sherry, beef and chicken broth; simmer 15 to 20 minutes.

In separate mixing bowl, whip together warm water and flour. Mix until smooth with no lumps remaining. Bring broth to a near boil. While whipping hot broth briskly, slowly add water-flour mixture. Reduce heat and simmer 20 to 30 minutes, stirring often to prevent scorching. Again whipping broth, slowly add cheeses, continue mixing until cheese is fully melted and suspended in soup. Slowly add cream and seasonings, simmer 15 minutes, stirring often. Taste and adjust seasonings if desired.

Makes 10 servings.

Casimiro Vega has been cooking up traditional Cuban food at this unpretentious eatery for more than 15 years.

Vega's Cafe's Black Bean Soup
Orlando

1 pound dried black beans
1 green pepper, quartered
¼ cup olive oil
1 large onion, chopped
4 cloves garlic, chopped
1 green pepper, chopped
2 teaspoons salt
½ teaspoon black pepper
¼ teaspoon oregano
2 teaspoons sugar
¼ teaspoon cumin
3 bay leaves
3 tablespoons vinegar
2 tablespoons dry red wine
2 tablespoons olive oil
Rice cooked in desired
    portions
Chopped onions for garnish

Rinse black beans thoroughly. Soak overnight in 10 cups water. Save water from soaked beans so the black color will be retained.

Add green pepper to beans and water, then either pressure cook for 45 minutes or cook on top of stove for 2 hours or until beans are tender.

Heat olive oil and saute chopped onions, garlic and green peppers. Add mixture to beans along with spices. Cook for 1 hour.

Add vinegar, wine and olive oil before serving. Serve over rice and top with chopped onions

Makes 6 servings.

This is just one of chef-owner Louis Perrotte's special menu items. The eye-appealing color contrast is achieved by using two ladles to fill the serving bowl.

Le Coq au Vin's Pumpkin and Broccoli Soup
Orlando

Pumpkin soup:
2 tablespoons butter
1/4 cup chopped onion
1 medium leek, white bulb
   only, cut into 1-inch pieces
4 cups peeled, uncooked
   pumpkin, diced (24 ounces
   of solid-pack pumpkin may
   be substituted)
6 cups chicken broth (reduce
   chicken broth to 5 cups if
   canned pumpkin is used)
1 cup heavy whipping cream,
   heated

Broccoli soup:
4 cups chopped fresh broccoli
1/4 cup chopped onion
1 garlic clove, chopped
3 cups chicken broth
1 cup heavy whipping cream,
   heated

To make pumpkin soup, in a large saucepan or stockpot melt butter, add 1/4 cup chopped onion and leek, saute until transparent. Stir in diced pumpkin and 6 cups of chicken broth. Cook until tender, about 1 hour. Puree in the work bowl of a blender or food processor. Stir in 1 cup of hot whipping cream and season to taste.

To make broccoli soup, combine all ingredients except heavy whipping cream in a large saucepan. Simmer until tender, 10 to 15 minutes. Do not overcook. Puree broccoli mixture in the work bowl of a blender or food processor. Stir in hot cream, season to taste.

To serve, fill one ladle with pumpkin soup and another with broccoli soup. In tandem, slowly pour in both on opposite sides of a serving bowl.

Makes 8 servings.

Le Coq Au Vin
FRENCH STYLE CUISINE

Sleepy Hollow Tea Room's proprietor-host Cavelle Pawlack created this colorful concoction. It is easy to duplicate in the home kitchen.

Sleepy Hollow's Cream of Carrot Soup
Orlando

3 cups shredded or grated
   carrots
¼ cup chopped onion
¼ cup chopped celery
4 cups chicken broth
4 cups heavy whipping cream
Salt and white pepper to taste

In saucepan, combine first 4 ingredients; simmer until tender. Do not overcook; vegetables should retain texture. Remove from heat and reserve.

In a second saucepan, warm cream. Bring up to a boil, but do not allow to boil. Cream will thicken as it heats. At desired consistency, slowly stir in broth and vegetable mixture. Season to taste.

Makes 4 large servings.

This hearty soup is often served as a "soup of the day" menu choice at the charming Sleepy Hollow Tea Room.

Sleepy Hollow's Black Bean Soup
Orlando

2 cups dry black beans
Water to cover
2 ribs celery, diced
1 small onion, diced
2 carrots, diced
4 cups beef broth
½ cup diced ham
1 cup cooked rice
1 bay leaf
¼ teaspoon basil
¼ teaspoon oregano
¼ teaspoon thyme
Salt and pepper to taste

Rinse beans, cover with water and soak overnight according to package directions.

Place undrained beans (do not drain and cover with fresh water or the beans will lose color) in heavy-bottomed kettle or stockpot.

Stir in diced vegetables, beef broth and ham. Bring to boil, reduce heat and simmer for 30 minutes. Add cooked rice, seasonings, salt and pepper; return to boil and simmer about 2 hours or until tender.

Makes 8 large servings.

Le Coq au Vin has long been a favorite with Central Florida diners. In fact, it was voted the best French restaurant in the area in a "Palate Pleasers" poll.

Le Coq au Vin's Cream of Zucchini With Curry
Orlando

2 tablespoons unsalted butter
1 clove garlic, diced
1 medium onion, diced
3 medium zucchini, sliced
3 tablespoons curry powder
3 cups chicken stock
1 cup heavy cream
Salt and pepper to taste
Dried fried plantain chips,
  crumbled for garnish

Melt butter in large saucepan. Add onion, garlic and zucchini. Saute mixture for 3 to 5 minutes.

Stir in curry powder. Add chicken stock and simmer for 20 minutes. Add cream and simmer 5 minutes more.

In the work bowl of a blender or food processor, puree the soup mixture in batches.

Return soup to saucepan.

Add salt and pepper to taste; if thicker than desired, slowly thin with additional chicken stock.

Serve the soup hot or cold, garnished with crumbled fried plantain chips.

Makes 6 servings.

Recipe notes: The curry can be cut back to 1 tablespoon if desired. The recipe produces a thick, light green soup that can be served hot or cold.

This soup takes some advance preparation. The ingredients are available at most supermarkets and Asian grocery stores.

China Garden's Hot and Sour Soup
Orlando

8 lily bud mushrooms

8 black mushrooms

4 wood ear mushrooms

$1/8$ cup vegetable or peanut oil

4 ounces pork loin, lightly frozen and cut in matchstick-thin strips about $1^1/2$ inches long

1 ounce bamboo shoots, cut into strips

1 teaspoon sherry

$2^1/2$ cups chicken broth

$1/2$ cake tofu, sliced and cut into strips

2 teaspoons soy sauce

$1/2$ teaspoon salt

$1/4$ teaspoon pepper

$1/4$ cup white vinegar

Hot oil (soak 2 to 3 dry red peppers in water for 1 hour. Drain. Chop peppers very fine. Cook in $1/2$ cup of oil for 1 minute; reserve)

2 tablespoons cornstarch dissolved in small amount of water

1 egg, beaten

Dash of sesame oil

1 green onion, chopped

Soak black mushrooms, lily bud and wood ear mushrooms in warm water for 1 hour. Drain and cut into strips; set aside.

Heat vegetable or peanut oil over medium-high heat. Add shredded pork, mushrooms and bamboo shoots. Stir for about 30 seconds. Add sherry and broth; bring to a boil. Add tofu, soy sauce, salt, pepper, vinegar and 1 teaspoon hot oil.

Thicken soup with cornstarch mixture. Slowly add beaten egg, stir and continue cooking for 30 seconds.

Serve garnished with dash of sesame oil and chopped green onion.

Makes 2 generous servings.

Chef John Palinski broke down this recipe for home preparation. This creamy concoction is one of the most popular soups on the Pebbles menu.

Pebbles' Tomato Basil Soup
Lake Buena Vista, Longwood, Orlando, Winter Park

6 tablespoons unsalted butter
1 clove peeled garlic, crushed
5 tablespoons flour
6 cups chicken stock, heated
1 cup crushed tomatoes
½ cup tomato paste
1 teaspoon Spike All-Purpose Seasoning (available in health food stores and some supermarkets)
1 teaspoon Maggi Seasoning (available in most supermarkets)
½ cup finely chopped fresh basil
3 dashes Tabasco sauce
1 cup heavy cream

In large saucepan, melt butter, saute garlic. Remove garlic, stir in flour. Whisk together and cook 5 minutes over low heat; continue whisking and do not burn.

Whisk in hot chicken stock, whisk until smooth. Add tomato paste, crushed tomatoes, Spike, Maggi Seasoning and Tabasco. Simmer 20 minutes. Add basil, simmer 5 minutes. Stir in heavy cream. Serve garnished with croutons.

This lush soup takes a bit of doing to make, but the effort can be wonderfully satisfying.

Pebbles' Cream of Wild Mushroom Soup
Lake Buena Vista, Longwood, Orlando, Winter Park

2 sticks unsalted butter
2 cups all-purpose flour
1 gallon chicken stock
1 bay leaf
1 tablespoon Maggi Seasoning
4 dashes Tabasco sauce
Salt to taste
Pepper to taste
Granulated garlic to taste
1/2 pound cultivated American
    mushrooms, sliced
1/2 pound shiitake
    mushrooms, sliced
2 ounces dried chanterelle or
    morel mushrooms,
    rehydrated, sliced
6 shallots, finely diced
1 tablespoon butter
2 tablespoons sherry
2 tablespoons brandy
1 pint heavy cream

In large soup kettle or stockpot, melt butter, stir in flour until smooth to make a roux; simmer over low heat 30 to 45 minutes until pale golden.

Gradually stir in stock to make chicken veloute (sauce). Add bay leaf, Maggi, Tabasco, salt, pepper and granulated garlic. Simmer, stirring occasionally, for about an hour. Strain mixture and reserve.

In separate saucepan, melt 1 tablespoon butter, add mushrooms and diced shallots and saute. When desired color and tenderness is reached, deglaze the pan with sherry and brandy. Fold mixture into veloute.

Add heavy cream and heat soup to serving temperature.

Makes about 1^1/$_2$ gallons.

This Broccoli Cheese Soup is a rich and zesty variation of the restaurant's creamy broccoli soup. The recipe was developed by chef John Palinski.

Pebbles' Broccoli Cheese Soup
Lake Buena Vista, Longwood, Orlando, Winter Park

2 quarts chicken stock
2 sticks butter
4 tablespoons flour
1 onion finely chopped
2 bunches fresh broccoli,
    cleaned, stems peeled, and
    chopped into medium to
    fine pieces
1 teaspoon Tabasco sauce
1 tablespoon Spike (available
    in health food stores and
    most supermarkets)
1 tablespoon Maggi
    Seasoning (available in
    most supermarkets)
1 bay leaf
1½ cups grated American
    cheese, not imitation cheese
½ cup grated Asiago cheese
1 cup heavy cream

Heat chicken stock or broth in separate saucepan. Set aside. In large soup kettle or stockpot, melt butter. Add chopped onion and saute about 3 minutes, do not allow to brown. Slowly whip in flour to make a roux. Cook for 5 minutes over low heat, stirring carefully. Add hot stock, whipping constantly with wire whisk. Bring to a boil, reduce to a simmer stirring occasionally. Add bay leaf, broccoli and rest of seasonings. Simmer for 1 hour, stirring occasionally.

Stir in cheeses and simmer for 10 minutes, continuing to stir to blend well. Stir in cream and serve.

Makes 12 servings.

In this recipe, executive chef Tony Pace has created a delicious cream soup that get its flavor from pureed snow peas.

Pebbles' Cream of Snow Pea Soup
Lake Buena Vista, Longwood, Orlando, Winter Park

1 stick butter
3 tablespoons chopped
　shallots
1/2 cup flour
3/4 gallon chicken stock,
　heated
2 pounds fresh or frozen snow
　peas, trimmed, strings
　removed
1/8 teaspoon Tabasco sauce
1 tablespoon Maggi Seasoning
　(available in health food
　stores and most
　supermarkets)
Salt and white pepper to taste
1/4 cup lemon juice
1 pint heavy cream
1/4 pound uncooked snow pea
　pods, julienned, for garnish

In a large soup pot, melt butter, add chopped shallots and saute until transparent. Whisk in flour until smooth and cook over low heat 5 minutes to make a roux. Add hot chicken broth and whisk until all lumps are removed.

Stir in 2 pounds of trimmed snow peas, seasonings and lemon juice. Cook until pea pods are very soft.

In batches, place soup in food processor or blender and puree. Strain if desired.

Return mixture to soup pot and bring just to a boil. Stir in heavy cream, reduce heat and warm through. Adjust seasonings. Add julienned pea pods just before serving.

Makes about 1 gallon.

Chicken Pepper Pot is a Pebbles original. It was developed by executive chef Tony Pace. The restaurant serves a similar creation called Cream of Duck With Peppercorns.

Pebbles' Chicken Pepper Pot
Lake Buena Vista, Longwood, Orlando, Winter Park

1 large onion, diced
2 sticks butter or margarine
1 tablespoons cracked black pepper
1¼ cups flour
14 cups chicken broth
1 bay leaf
1 tablespoon Maggi Seasoning (available in most supermarkets)
1 tablespoon Spike Seasoning (available in health food stores and most supermarkets)
⅛ teaspoon cayenne pepper
1 teaspoon Tabasco sauce
1 red pepper, diced
1 green pepper, diced
1 pound cooked chicken meat, diced
2 tablespoons canned green peppercorns
1 pint whipping cream
2 cups cooked rice for garnish (optional)

In large saucepan or stockpot, saute onions in butter, add cracked black pepper and saute until onions are transparent. Stir in flour to make a roux, cook over low heat, stirring occasionally, for about 15 minutes.

Whip in hot chicken broth or stock. Whip until roux is thoroughly dissolved. Add bay leaf, Maggi, Spike, green peppercorns, cayenne pepper and Tabasco. Cook mixture for 15 minutes. Stir in red and green peppers and diced chicken. Simmer for 30 minutes, stirring occasionally. Stir in cream. Remove pan from heat as soon as soup warms cream.

To serve, ladle into individual serving bowls and garnish with cooked rice.

Makes 16 servings.

For maximum flavor, follow the directions carefully and use a good brand of balsamic vinegar. This aged vinegar is available in supermarkets and specialty food shops.

Pebbles' Lentil Soup With Kielbasa
Lake Buena Vista, Longwood, Orlando, Winter Park

1 medium yellow onion
3 medium carrots
3 ribs celery
1½ sticks unsalted butter
About ¾ cup flour
1 gallon chicken stock, heated
1 pound washed and picked
   over lentils
Sweet ham bone or 1 ounce
   ham base
1 bay leaf
Salt and black pepper to taste
1 (12-ounce) can tomatoes,
   ground
¼ ounce Maggi Seasoning
   (available in health food
   stores and most
   supermarkets)
1 pound smoked kielbasa
   sausage, diced
⅓ cup balsamic vinegar

Dice onion, carrots and celery into medium pieces. Saute in large soup kettle or Dutch oven with unsalted butter until tender. Stir in flour and cook 10 minutes over medium heat, stirring occasionally.

Add hot chicken stock and whip with wire whisk until all lumps are removed. Bring mixture to a boil and stir in lentils, ham bone, bay leaf, salt, pepper, tomatoes and Maggi Seasoning. Reduce heat to simmer and cook gently for 45 minutes to 1 hour. Stir occasionally. Add diced kielbasa and simmer 10 more minutes.

Stir in balsamic vinegar just before serving.

Makes about 1 gallon.

Sleepy Hollow Tea Room's creamy rendition of the old American BLT sandwich is remarkably simple to make at home.

Sleepy Hollow's Cream of BLT Soup
Orlando

1 cup chicken broth
½ cup chopped lettuce
    (iceberg, romaine, leaf or
    any combination)
½ cup diced tomatoes
¼ cup chopped onion
¼ cup chopped celery
1 cup heavy whipping cream
2 teaspoons sherry
1 teaspoon sugar
Salt and pepper to taste

In a large saucepan or stock pot, combine broth with lettuce, diced tomatoes, bacon, onions and celery. Bring mixture to a boil, reduce the heat, cover and simmer for 20 minutes.

Stir in heavy cream, sherry, sugar and salt and pepper to taste. Simmer, stirring, until cream content thickens soup to desired consistency.

Makes 5 servings.

Sleepy Hollow
Gifts & Tea Room

This mushroom soup from Sleepy Hollow Tea Room is best when made in advance, giving the flavors a chance to meld.

Sleepy Hollow's Cream of Mushroom Soup
Orlando

2 cups fresh mushrooms,
   cleaned
3/4 cup chopped green onions,
   bulbs and tops
1/4 cup butter
2 tablespoons flour
1 cup chicken stock or broth
1 cup half-and-half
Salt and pepper to taste
1/2 cup Burgundy wine

Finely chop mushrooms. In a large saucepan, saute mushrooms and green onions in butter until tender. Stir in flour and continue cooking, stirring continuously, about 3 minutes.

Remove pan from heat. Slowly whisk in chicken broth and half-and-half. Return pan to heat. Add salt and pepper to taste and Burgundy. Reheat to serve.

Makes 4 servings.

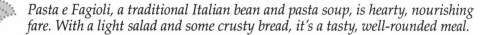

Pasta e Fagioli, a traditional Italian bean and pasta soup, is hearty, nourishing fare. With a light salad and some crusty bread, it's a tasty, well-rounded meal.

Village Restaurant's Pasta e Fagioli
Disney Village Marketplace, Lake Buena Vista

½ pound Great Northern
   beans
2 ham hocks, cut in pieces
2½ tablespoons finely
   chopped onion
2 tablespoons finely chopped
   carrots
½ cup canned plum tomatoes
   chopped with juice
3 cups chicken broth
Salt to taste
Fresh ground pepper to taste
1 cup uncooked macaroni
   (elbows, shells or bow ties)
Freshly grated Parmesan
   cheese

Cover beans with water and soak overnight. Wash and drain in the morning. Put beans in a large saucepan or stockpot with ham hock pieces and cover with water (about 1 inch above beans).

Bring to boil and simmer 45 minutes, covered. Drain beans and return to pan. Do not remove ham hocks. Add vegetables, tomatoes and chicken broth. Bring mixture to a boil and cook, covered, for 20 to 25 minutes or until beans are tender.

When ham hocks are cooked, remove from pot and cool enough to remove bone and fat. Dice meat and set aside.

Remove ½ cup of the beans from the pot and mash. Return to soup. Season soup to taste with salt and pepper.

Add more chicken broth, if necessary, so soup will not be too thick. Add macaroni and diced ham and cook for 10 minutes. Let soup rest for 10 minutes before serving. Serve with Parmesan cheese.

Makes 2 quarts.

Lord Chumley's Pub was a favorite dining spot on State Road 436 in Altamonte Springs. The restaurant was well-known for its hearty food.

Lord Chumley's Hungarian Goulash Soup
Altamonte Springs

1 stick butter
¹/₂ cup chopped onions
¹/₂ cup chopped bell pepper
1 pound pork tenderloin, cubed
1 pound beef tenderloin, cubed
1¹/₂ tablespoons paprika
Water
1 cup sliced carrots
4 tomatoes, quartered
¹/₂ teaspoon cumin
8 to 9 drops Tabasco sauce
¹/₂ teaspoon black pepper
¹/₂ teaspoon white pepper
¹/₄ teaspoon garlic powder
2 tablespoons beef base or instant beef bouillon
4 to 5 potatoes, cubed

In a Dutch oven or soup kettle, saute in butter the onion, bell pepper, pork, beef and paprika until well browned. Measure out enough water to barely cover (measure amount of water used because the amount is tripled in the final cooking stage). Add carrots, tomatoes, cumin, Tabasco, peppers, garlic powder and beef base. Simmer 40 minutes. Add water (three times more than the original amount) and potatoes. Stir and simmer until potatoes are tender.

Makes 8 servings.

There are a number of variations of this hearty soup. Perhaps the most famous concoction is the soup that is served in the U.S. Senate dining room. There is also a House of Representatives version on page 54. Take your pick.

U.S. Senate's Bean Soup
Washington, D.C.

2 pounds dry Great Northern beans
4 cups water
1 pound ham bone, cut in sections
½ cup chopped onions
2 medium carrots, thinly sliced
2 ribs celery, chopped
⅛ teaspoon prepared mustard
⅛ cup minced green pepper
½ cup tomato puree
1 whole clove
2 peppercorns

Wash beans thoroughly. Cover beans with water and soak for 12 hours, drain. Place all ingredients in a large soup kettle or stockpot, season to taste with salt and pepper.

Simmer mixture for 4 hours, stirring occasionally and adding liquid if necessary. Remove ham bones, serve with crackers.

Makes 8 servings.

If the U.S. Senate Bean Soup doesn't suit you, try this simple preparation from the House of Representatives dining room.

House of Representatives' Bean Soup
Washington, D.C.

---

2 pounds white Michigan beans
Smoked ham hock
Salt and pepper to taste

Wash beans and soak overnight in cold water. Drain beans and cover with fresh water. Add ham hock and simmer slowly for about 4 hours until beans are cooked tender. Add salt and pepper to taste.

Just before serving, bruise beans with a large spoon or ladle, enough to cloud liquid.

Makes 6 servings.

King Henry's Feast is a family dinner-show attraction located on International Drive in Orlando. It's popular with locals as well as tourists.

King Henry's Feast's Leek and Potato Soup
Orlando

1 cup chopped fresh leeks
1 cup peeled and diced
 potatoes
½ cup chopped onions
2 teaspoons fresh chopped
 parsley
⅓ cup finely chopped celery
¼ teaspoon salt
¼ teaspoon celery salt
¼ teaspoon celery seed
⅛ teaspoon white pepper
2 cubes chicken bouillon
2 cups water
½ gallon milk
1 pint half-and-half
½ cup instant potato granules

Put vegetables, seasonings and bouillon in a kettle with water. Simmer until vegetables are tender. Stir in milk and half-and-half. Heat slowly to serving temperature. Do not boil. Cream-based soups will curdle if heated too quickly.

Add instant potatoes to thicken. Makes 12 servings.

Chamberlin's Natural Foods has been the health-conscious cook's friend for many years. The store stocks whole grains, seasonings and deli items.

Chamberlin's Cheese and Broccoli Soup
Altamonte Springs, Casselberry, Orlando, Winter Park

1/3 cup chopped onion
1 clove garlic, minced
1/3 cup chopped celery or
    celery leaves
1 tablespoon olive oil
2 teaspoons Spike Seasoning
    (available in supermarkets
    and health food stores)
2 teaspoons bouillon granules
    or vegetable base
1/2 tablespoon dried parsley
    flakes
1 teaspoon basil leaves
1/2 teaspoon thyme
1/8 teaspoon white pepper
1 bunch broccoli, about
    1 1/2 pounds
1 1/3 pounds potatoes, skins
    on, scrubbed and diced
Water
1/2 pound Monterey Jack
    cheese, grated
1/2 cup milk

In a stockpot or large saucepan, saute onions and celery in olive oil until tender. Turn heat to low and add all spices and herbs. Stir and let stand for 1 minute.

Chop broccoli stems and leaves, reserving florets.

Add chopped broccoli and diced potatoes to spice mixture. Cover with water and bring to a boil. Simmer mixture for 20 minutes.

Break up and steam florets; set aside.

Blend soup in the work bowl of a blender or food processor until creamy. You may need to do this in batches. Return soup to pot. Add cheese, milk, steamed florets. Heat mixture thoroughly but do not boil.

Makes 5 (12-ounce) servings.

Barney's Steak & Seafood has been a fixture on Orlando's Colonial Drive for years. Besides serving fabulous steaks, the restaurant is also known for its delicious soups and salads.

Barney's Cream of Whatever Soup
Orlando

1½ pounds cauliflower, fresh
   spinach, broccoli (including
   stems), carrots, cabbage or
   potatoes, diced
1½ quarts water
½ stick butter
1 medium onion, diced
4 ounces flour
4 cubes chicken bouillon
2 cups half-and-half
Salt and pepper to taste

In a 2-quart saucepan, combine diced vegetable of choice with water. Simmer for about 1½ hours. Remove pan from heat.

In another large saucepan or stockpot, melt butter and saute onions until transparent. Add flour and blend well.

Add vegetables (including cooking water), bouillon cubes. Blend together until mixture thickens. Simmer for 5 minutes, stirring occasionally. Stir in half-and-half and salt and pepper to taste.

Makes 8 servings.

Recipe notes: For cauliflower soup, add a pinch of fennel. For spinach and broccoli soup, add ⅛ teaspoon of garlic powder. For cabbage soup, add a spice bag (¼ teaspoon mixed pickling spices wrapped in cheesecloth) to simmering liquid. For potato soup, add ¼ cup diced cooked celery and ½ teaspoon celery seed.

Gus' Villa Rosa on Orlando's Old Winter Garden Road is a charming Italian eatery. From appetizers to desserts, the menu offers something for everyone.

Gus' Villa Rosa's Crab Soup
Orlando

$\frac{1}{2}$ cup finely chopped onions
$\frac{1}{4}$ pound butter, divided
1 cup blue, king or snow crab pieces
1 cup fish stock or 1 teaspoon fish base
$\frac{1}{4}$ cup sherry
2 (14-ounce) cans cream of celery soup
2 cups half-and-half
2 pinches mace
1 tablespoon arrowroot or cornstarch (optional)
1 tablespoon fresh parsley, finely chopped

In a large saucepan or stockpot, saute onions with half of the butter. When onions are translucent, add crab meat and cook slowly. Add fish stock or base. Cook for 2 minutes. Add sherry to mixture and simmer for 1 minute. Remove pan from heat.

In another saucepan, dilute cream of celery soup with half-and-half. Stir in mace. Slowly heat celery soup mixture and then add to fish stock mixture.

If needed, thicken with arrowroot or cornstarch. The consistency of the soup should be similar to heavy cream. Add parsley. Dot individual servings with remaining butter.

Makes 4 to 6 cups.

This variation of a basic oyster stew was developed by former Church Street executive chef Michael Orr. Crackers' chef Al Alvarado goes heavier on the ground pepper than salt which gives the creamy stew a more robust taste.

Crackers' Oyster Stew
Church Street Station, Orlando

½ cup heavy cream
½ cup milk
Salt and ground pepper to taste
2 tablespoons chopped scallions
3 dashes Tabasco or Crystal hot sauce
Fresh oysters with natural juice
1 teaspoon butter

In a saucepan, combine heavy cream, milk, salt and pepper, chopped scallions, and hot sauce.

Over medium heat, cook for 1 minute, stirring constantly.

Add oysters and juice and butter. Stir and continue simmering for 2 more minutes. Do not allow to boil.

Oyster Stew should be warm, not blazing hot.

Serve immediately.

Makes 1 serving.

This chowder is just one of the many specialties Jim and Sheila Alexander prepare at this downtown Orlando restaurant. The menu includes vegetarian and low-fat items, fruit breads, rich soups, sandwiches and entrees.

Thornton Park Cafe's Corn and Crab Chowder
Orlando

Bechamel sauce:
1 cup milk
½ cup flour
3 cups milk
½ pound onion, chopped
½ stick butter
½ teaspoon white pepper
1 tablespoon salt
¼ teaspoon nutmeg
¼ teaspoon thyme

Chowder:
4 cups corn kernels scraped from cob to obtain all juices from the ear of corn (frozen corn kernels may be substituted)
1 red bell pepper, finely diced
2 green onions, thinly sliced
¼ teaspoon chili powder
½ teaspoon salt
½ teaspoon black pepper
1 teaspoon finely diced jalapeno pepper
1 cup half-and-half
10 ounces cooked crab meat

To make bechamel sauce, blend 1 cup milk and ½ cup flour with a whisk until thoroughly mixed. Heat 3 cups milk in microwave oven on high (100 percent) power for 4 minutes.

Transfer milk to a pot and place over medium heat on stovetop. Slowly add the flour-milk mixture, stirring with whisk. Stir until thickened and smooth.

In a saucepan, cook onion, butter, white pepper, salt, nutmeg and thyme over medium-low heat until onions are translucent. Do not allow onions to brown. Puree the onion mixture with 1 cup of the milk mixture in a blender or food processor. When pureed, return to the pan and blend together; set aside.

In a food processor or blender, chop fine 2 cups of the corn kernels. Put chopped corn mixture and all remaining ingredients except crab meat into a stockpot. Cook over medium-low heat until corn is tender and liquid has reduced to creamed corn consistency. Pick over cooked crab meat to remove any shell fragments or cartilage.

Stir reserved bechamel sauce into chowder. Blend in cooked crab.

Makes about 10 servings.

Here's another delicious soup from Pebbles' fabulous menu. Chef Tony Pace has blended artichokes and mushrooms to may this creamy concoction.

Pebbles' Artichoke & Mushroom Soup
Lake Buena Vista, Longwood, Orlando, Winter Park

2 sticks unsalted butter or
    margarine
1 cup all-purpose flour
1 pound mushrooms, sliced
3 tablespoons butter or
    margarine
3 quarts chicken stock,
    warmed
1 bay leaf
1 tablespoon Maggi Seasoning
4 dashes Tabasco
1 tablespoon Spike Seasoning
    (available at health food and
    some grocery stores)
Salt and white pepper to taste
2 (14-ounce) cans artichoke
    hearts (not marinated),
    drained and diced
1 pint heavy cream

In a large soup kettle, melt unsalted margarine or butter. Whisk in flour and cook over low heat for about 15 minutes, stirring occasionally.

Saute mushrooms in 3 tablespoons of butter or margarine. When mushrooms are soft, set aside.

Add warm chicken stock to butter and flour mixture. Whisk until stock is lump-free. Stir in all seasonings and simmer for 15 minutes.

Add sauteed mushrooms and diced artichokes hearts. Simmer for 15 minutes. Blend in heavy cream. Serve warm.

Makes about 1 gallon.

Salads &
Dressings

Moorefield's restaurant in downtown Orlando offers an eclectic menu and a cozy wine bar.

Moorefield's Citrus Raspberry Salad
Orlando

4 heads hydroponic Bibb lettuce
2 cups sliced, fresh strawberries
2 oranges cut into segments,
    membranes removed
1/2 cup walnuts, lightly chopped
1 lemon, juiced

Raspberry vinaigrette:
2/3 cup extra-virgin olive oil
1/3 cup raspberry vinegar

Raspberry simple syrup:
1 cup fresh raspberries
Juice of 1/2 lemon
2 tablespoons Port

To make simple syrup, bring fresh raspberries, juice of 1/2 lemon and Port to a boil. Cook mixture until volume is reduced by half and mixture begins to thicken. Remove from heat and cool to room temperature.

In the work bowl of a food processor, blend olive oil and raspberry vinegar. Add simple syrup mixture and remaining lemon juice. Blend until vinaigrette is thoroughly combined.

Arrange lettuce leaves on 6 salad plates. Pour vinaigrette over lettuce. Divide orange segments, strawberry slices and walnuts among serving plates.

Makes 6 servings.

Gary's Duck Inn is considered the granddaddy of Orlando seafood restaurants. It has been a fixture in south Orlando for many years.

Gary's Duck Inn's Cole Slaw
Orlando

$^2/_3$ cup granulated sugar
Dash of salt
Pinch black pepper
Pinch celery seed
1 teaspoon prepared mustard
$2^1/_2$ ounces cider vinegar
13 ounces mayonnaise (not
   salad dressing)
1 tablespoon fresh lemon juice
$^3/_4$ pound green cabbage, finely
   chopped
$^1/_2$ large carrot, grated

In a large bowl, mix together all ingredients except cabbage and grated carrot. Stir in cabbage and carrot and refrigerate to chill. Mixture will keep well in refrigerator.

Makes 4 servings.

This recipe was developed by Gary Spruce, deli manager of the Lake Howell Square Chamberlin's.

Chamberlin's Eggless Egg Salad
Altamonte Springs, Casselberry, Orlando, Winter Park

1 pound tofu
$\frac{1}{2}$ teaspoon granulated garlic
$\frac{1}{2}$ teaspoon sea salt
2 tablespoons dried chopped
   onions
4 ribs celery, finely chopped
2 tablespoons pickle relish
   (optional)
Fresh parsley for garnish

Tofu mayonnaise:
$\frac{1}{2}$ cup crumbled tofu
$\frac{1}{4}$ cup water
$\frac{1}{4}$ cup canola oil
1 tablespoon mustard
1 tablespon sea salt
$\frac{1}{2}$ teaspoon turmeric

In a large bowl, crumble tofu with hands or potato masher. Stir in garlic, sea salt, chopped onions, celery and pickle relish.

Put all ingredients for tofu mayonnaise in the work bowl of a blender or food processor. Mix ingredients to bind. Makes about $\frac{3}{4}$ cup.

Blend tofu mayonnaise with other salad ingredients.

Garnish with parsley.

Makes 6 sandwiches.

This salad has been one of Cavelle Pawlack's hottest sellers at the quaint Sleepy Hollow Tea Room. The salad is best served right after preparing. Turkey may be substituted for chicken.

Sleepy Hollow's Chicken Salad Supreme
Orlando

4 cups diced cooked chicken
³/₄ cup dark or golden raisins
³/₄ cup drained pineapple
   tidbits
1 teaspoon Dijon mustard
1 teaspoon curry powder
³/₄ cup mayonnaise
¹/₃ cup chopped celery
Lettuce
¹/₂ cup chopped pecans
Fresh grapes for garnish

In a large bowl, blend together chicken, raisins, pineapple, mustard, curry powder, mayonnaise and celery.

Place four large servings on bed of lettuce. Top each serving with chopped pecans. Garnish with grapes and serve with fresh fruit.

Makes 4 servings.

Pebbles' Caesar Salad
Lake Buena Vista, Longwood, Orlando, Winter Park

1 small head romaine lettuce
Dash salt
Dash red-wine vinegar
$1/2$ cup croutons
Cracked black pepper to taste
$1/4$ cup grated Parmesan cheese

Caesar dressing:
$1/4$ teaspoon anchovies
$1/8$ teaspoon dry mustard
1 coddled egg yolk
$1/8$ teaspoon fresh garlic
$1/8$ teaspoon lemon juice
2 dashes Worcestershire sauce
2 dashes Tabasco
$1/8$ cup plus 1 tablespoon red-wine vinegar
3 tablespoons olive oil
Cracked black pepper to taste

In a wood bowl, work anchovies into a paste with a fork. Stir in mustard and coddled yolk. Whisk in garlic, lemon juice, Worcestershire, Tabasco, and $1/8$ cup vinegar. Gradually whisk in olive oil. As mixture thickens, dilute with remaining vinegar. Add pepper. Makes about 1 pint.

Wash and clean romaine by soaking leaves briefly in cool water that has been splashed with a dash of salt and red-wine vinegar. Drain leaves. Refrigerate leaves for several hours to crisp. Cut lettuce into 1-inch squares, trim and discard heavy ribs on outer leaves. Put in bowl and toss with enough dressing to coat leaves. Add croutons, pepper and cheese.

Makes 2 large portions.

Recipe notes: Coddling involves placing the food in a container that is covered, set in a larger pan of simmering water and cooked on low heat. Coddling will not kill salmonella. The lemon juice and vinegar in the dressing can hinder the growth of the salmonella. Egg substitutes may be used as an alternative.

Caesar salad is one of two dinner salad choices offered at Caruso's Palace, the elegant Italian restaurant in south Orlando. The dressing was developed by executive chef Arch Maynard and sous-chef Mark Crook.

Caruso's Palace's Caesar Salad
Orlando

3 uncooked egg yolks (see note)
1 tablespoon Dijon mustard
1/2 tablespoon Worcestershire sauce
3 1/2 tablespoons lemon juice
1 1/2 ounces red-wine vinegar
5 anchovy fillets, crushed
1 tablespoon crushed garlic
1 1/2 ounces grated Parmesan cheese
6 ounces olive oil
Salt and black pepper to taste
2 heads romaine lettuce, cleaned, torn into bite-size pieces and chilled
Grated Parmesan cheese for garnish

Garlic croutons:
1 clove garlic, diced
4 tablespoons butter, at room temperature
4 slices white bread, crusts trimmed
Grated Parmesan cheese

In a medium-size bowl, whip egg yolks. Beat in mustard, Worcestershire, lemon juice and red-wine vinegar. Add anchovies, garlic and grated Parmesan cheese. Slowly blend in olive oil, stirring constantly.

Preheat oven to 350F.

To make garlic croutons, blend diced garlic into butter. Spread on bread slices. Cut bread into cubes and bake in oven until bread cubes are toasty, stirring midway through baking. Remove croutons from oven. Before the croutons cool completely, sprinkle with grated Parmesan to taste.

In a large bowl, toss romaine with dressing and garlic croutons. Garnish with grated Parmesan. Season salad to taste with salt and pepper.

Makes 8 servings.

Recipe notes: Eggs should be kept refrigerated until ready to use. The lemon juice and vinegar in the Caesar dressing can hinder the growth of salmonella, if it is present. Egg substitutes, which are pasteurized (a process that destroys salmonella bacteria), may be used as a raw egg alternative.

Sybil Spath, proprietor of Maison des Crepes – an intimate little restaurant in Park Avenue's Hidden Gardens – provided this recipe. There is no oil in chef Robert Howe's vinaigrette.

Maison des Crepes' Melon Salad Vinaigrette
Winter Park

2 cups red-wine vinegar
1¼ cups granulated sugar
¼ teaspoon granulated
  garlic
¼ teaspoon ground white
  pepper

To prepare vinaigrette, combine ingredients in saucepan that will hold at least 4 cups of liquid. Bring mixture to a boil. Remove pan from heat, let stand at room temperature for 30 minutes. Pour dressing in a storage container and chill.

While dressing is chilling, cut slices of cantaloupe and honeydew for as many salads as needed. When vinaigrette is chilled, add fruit slices and marinate 15 to 30 minutes. Remove melon from dressing and arrange on bed of romaine lettuce. Garnish with a tomato wedge and a slice of cucumber.

Makes enough for 6 to 8 salads.

Sweetwater Country Club's executive chef Fred Mildner created this simple salad.

Sweetwater Country Club's Chicken Salad
Apopka

3 pounds boneless, skinless
   chicken breasts
2 ribs celery, finely diced
2 tablespoons chopped, fresh
   tarragon, or 1 tablespoon
   dried
1 cup mayonnaise
Pinch of white pepper
Mixed greens of choice
Fresh fruit or vegetables for
   garnish

Poaching liquid:
2 quarts water
1 rib celery, finely chopped
$\frac{1}{2}$ peeled onion
Butter or vegetable oil

To make poaching liquid, saute onion and chopped celery rib in a small amount of butter or vegetable oil for 5 minutes. Add water and simmer for 20 minutes. Add chicken breasts, return mixture to a boil then reduce heat and simmer for 30 minutes. Remove chicken from pan and cool completely.

Cut chicken into $\frac{1}{2}$-inch dice. Add diced celery, tarragon, mayonnaise and white pepper. Mix well.

Serve on a bed of greens garnished with fresh fruit or vegetables.

Makes 6 servings.

Sunflower seeds, almonds and walnuts give this salad a hearty crunch. The vinaigrette can be served on other salad combinations.

Pebbles' Nutty Cheesy Salad
Lake Buena Vista, Longwood, Orlando, Winter Park

½ head romaine lettuce, cut
   in 1-inch squares
¼ head iceberg lettuce, cut in
   1-inch squares
½ cup grated Cheddar cheese
½ cup chopped Danish
   fontina cheese
½ cup sunflower seeds
½ cup sliced almonds
½ cup chopped walnuts

Garnish:
½ tomato, quartered
1 teaspoon black olive slices
Salad Gems (available in
   health food stores)

Vinaigrette dressing:
1 (8-ounce) jar Dijon mustard
2 tablespoons dry mustard
4 tablespoons oregano
4 tablespoons granulated
   garlic
2 tablespoons paprika
½ tablespoon cracked black
   pepper
½ tablespoon salt
⅔ cup of sugar
Scant ⅓ cup lemon juice
Scant ⅓ cup soy sauce
1 quart salad oil
2 cups red-wine vinegar

To make dressing, in a small bowl, blend Dijon mustard with dry mustard. Add spices, sugar and lemon juice. Slowly whisk in soy sauce, oil and vinegar.

Cover dressing and store in the refrigerator.

Makes about 1½ quarts.

Combine lettuce squares. Line individual salad bowls with the lettuce mixture.

Combine the cheeses and put in center of lettuce squares.

Combine the nuts and sprinkle around cheese mixture.

Garnish with tomato wedges. Place olive slices in center of cheese mix and sprinkle with Salad Gems.

To serve, toss at table with vinaigrette dressing to taste.

Makes 1 serving.

Park Plaza Gardens' dramatic tableside preparation of this fabulous Caesar salad was developed by chef Philippe M. Gehin.

Park Plaza Gardens' Caesar Salad for Four
Winter Park

2 cloves garlic
4 fillets of anchovies, drained
3 tablespoons Dijon mustard
Pinch of salt
Pinch of freshly ground
   pepper
2 egg yolks
2 tablespoons Worcestershire
   sauce
¼ cup champagne or white
   vinegar
¾ cup olive oil
1 cup grated Parmesan cheese
1 head romaine lettuce,
   washed, patted dry, and
   chopped
2 cups toasted croutons
   flavored with paprika,
   oregano and garlic

In a large salad bowl, crush together the garlic cloves and anchovies. Mix in mustard, salt, pepper and egg yolks. Add Worcestershire sauce and vinegar. Slowly whisk in the oil. Add Parmesan cheese, lettuce and croutons.

Toss well and serve.

Makes 4 servings.

PARK PLAZA
GARDENS

Restaurant owner Cavelle Pawlack developed the following simple, vegetable-rich salad. Sleepy Hollow Tea Room is open for lunch Monday through Saturday.

Sleepy Hollow's Broccoli Carrot Salad
Orlando

1 large bunch broccoli
1 cup shredded carrots
1 cup chopped yellow onions
1 cup raisins
1 cup mayonnaise
1 (8-ounce) container low-fat
  plain yogurt
1/4 cup white vinegar
1/2 cup sugar
1/2 teaspoon black pepper

Trim and cut broccoli into small pieces.

In a large bowl, combine carrots, onions, broccoli, raisins and mayonnaise.

In another bowl, blend yogurt, vinegar, sugar and pepper. Stir yogurt mixture into vegetable mixture. Refrigerate at least an hour before serving. Serve in small bowls.

Makes 5 servings.

Chef Miguel Serrano's unusual spinach salad is a favorite of theatergoers. The Mark Two Dinner Theater is located in Orlando's College Park area.

Mark Two's Spinach Salad
Orlando

3 pounds frozen spinach, thawed and squeezed very dry
3 hard-boiled eggs, shredded
1 cup shredded Cheddar cheese
1 cup mayonnaise
1/4 cup Gulden's brown mustard
1 teaspoon salt
1 teaspoon lemon juice
1/2 teaspoon Tabasco Sauce
Pinch white pepper
1 teaspoon soy sauce
Pinch onion powder
Hard-boiled egg quarters (optional)
Chopped green onions (optional)

In a large bowl, blend together all ingredients. Chill 2 hours. If desired, garnish with hard-boiled egg quarters and chopped scallions.

Makes 6 servings.

The caraway seed flavoring adds zest to this hearty dish. The salad is best when the flavors are allowed to meld overnight in the refrigerator.

Captain Appleby's Reuben Salad
Mount Dora

2 pounds shredded sauerkraut,
   drained
1/3 cup sugar
3/4 cup mayonnaise
2 tablespoons caraway seeds

Thousand Island dressing:
1 quart mayonnaise
3/4 jar chili sauce
5 hard-boiled eggs, grated
1/8 cup sugar
1/8 cup salad oil
1/8 cup vinegar
6 tablespoons pickle relish
1 teaspoon relish liquid
1/8 cup grated onion

To make dressing, in a medium-size bowl, combine all dressing ingredients.
   Makes 1 quart of dressing.
   In a large bowl, toss salad ingredients with desired amount of Thousand Island dressing. Refrigerate overnight.
   Makes 8 servings.

The Silver Lake Golf & Country Club in Leesburg offers this salad dressing daily. It is also on the banquet menu.

Silver Lake's Oriental Sweet Sour Dressing
Leesburg

1½ cups red-wine vinegar
⅛ cup cider vinegar
1½ tablespoons soy sauce
1½ cups light brown sugar, firmly packed
½ teaspoon cayenne pepper
1 tablespoon dry mustard
1 teaspoon brown ginger powder
1 teaspoon salt
1 cup vegetable salad oil

In medium-size saucepan, combine red-wine and cider vinegars and soy sauce. Heat mixture over medium heat, but do not boil. When hot, remove pan from stove and add brown sugar. Mix until sugar is completely dissolved.

Add remaining ingredients and mix well. Refrigerate dressing in a storage container until ready to serve.

Whisk dressing right before serving.

Recipe notes: The restaurant serves this dressing with torn fresh spinach leaves, sliced mushrooms and toasted or untoasted sesame seeds. Mix with desired amount of dressing. Refrigerate remaining dressing.

Makes 1½ pints.

This unusual tangy treat adds flavor to fruit salads. It's even better if the flavors are allowed to meld overnight in the refrigerator.

Omni International's Cinnamon Dressing
Orlando

8 ounces of yogurt

4 ounces sour cream

2 ounces of Coco Lopez (cream of coconut)

1½ teaspoons powdered cinnamon

In a small bowl, combine all ingredients.

Toss with your favorite Waldorf salad combination or fruit salad.

Makes 6 to 8 servings.

The Bakerstreet chain has closed but many people still remember the restaurant's hearty salads and flavorful dressings.

Bakerstreet's Blue Cheese Dressing
Orlando

32 ounces (2 pounds) sour
  cream
2 quarts mayonnaise
$\frac{1}{2}$ cup tarragon vinegar
  (available in gourmet shops
  and some supermarkets)
$\frac{1}{2}$ tablespoon granulated
  garlic
$\frac{1}{4}$ teaspoon salt
$\frac{1}{4}$ tablespoon black pepper
1 cup buttermilk
$\frac{2}{3}$ pound blue cheese

In a large bowl, combine all ingredients except cheese.

When throughly blended, crumble cheese into mixture. Stir in lightly so that crumbles are not crushed.

Refrigerate dressing, tightly covered, until ready to serve.

The White Horse Saloon is the Hyatt Regency Grand Cypress' fun watering hole. The menu features Black Angus steaks and free-range grilled chicken. Dinners are often accompanied by a salad with this dressing.

White Horse Saloon's Applesauce Dressing
Hyatt Regency Grand Cypress, Lake Buena Vista

¼ cup soy bean salad oil
2 tablespoons corn syrup
2 tablespoons vinegar
2 tablespoons Worcestershire
  sauce
2 tablespoons sherry
2 egg yolks, beaten
⅛ cup applesauce
2 tablespoons tomato paste
2 tablespoons chopped fresh
  garlic
2 tablespoons soy sauce

In a medium-size bowl, whisk together ingredients until well blended. Refrigerate until ready to serve.

Serve drizzled over salad greens of choice.

Makes 3 to 4 servings.

HYATT REGENCY ✿ GRAND CYPRESS

The Miliotes family is at the helm of Chris's House of Beef. The John Young Parkway restaurant is a popular spot for special occasion dinners.

House of Beef's Honey Mustard Dressing
Orlando

2 tablespoons Pommery
    whole-grain mustard
5 ounces olive or vegetable oil
3 tablespoons cider vinegar
 1 teaspoon honey

Put all ingredients in the work bowl of a blender. Blend for about 1 minute.

Makes 1 cup.

81

The Lakeside Inn is an historic waterfront hotel and restaurant located near Mount Dora's quaint downtown shopping area. The Beauclaire dining room serves lunch, dinner and Sunday brunch.

Lakeside Inn's Honey Mustard Dressing
Mount Dora

1 pint mayonnaise
1 pint prepared yellow
   mustard
¼ pound light brown sugar
1 pint honey
Dash Tabasco sauce
Dash Worcestershire sauce
4 tablespoons poppy seeds

In a medium-size bowl, blend all ingredients thoroughly. Refrigerate for at least 1 hour before serving.
Makes about 1 quart.

This dressing is usually drizzled over a mixture of lettuce, mushrooms and pimento or red pepper.

Le Coq au Vin's French Mustard Dressing
Orlando

1 egg yolk
1 tablespoon chopped shallots
1 teaspoon chopped garlic
3 ounces red-wine vinegar
1 tablespoon Grey Poupon
   Mustard
2 tablespoons country-style
   Dijon mustard with seeds
1 cup olive oil
1 cup peanut oil
2 teaspoons warm water

In an electric mixer bowl, combine egg yolk, shallot, garlic, vinegar and mustards. At low speed, pour oils very slowly so they will blend smoothly in egg and mustard mixture. Add more vinegar if needed. Then add warm water slowly until desired consistency is reached. Dressing should be consistency of cream. Cover dressing and refrigerate until ready to serve.

Makes about $2^1/2$ cups.

This is just one of many dressing choices offered at Straub's Fine Seafood. It can also be warmed and used as a sauce for fish.

Straub's Honey Mustard Dressing
Altamonte Springs, Orlando

¼ cup plus 1 tablespoon Dijon
  mustard
¼ cup plus 1 tablespoon apple-
  cider vinegar
1 quart mayonnaise
1 teaspoon white pepper
1 teaspoon paprika
¼ teaspoon cayenne pepper
1 cup honey

Mix together mustard, vinegar, mayonnaise, white pepper, paprika, and cayenne.

Warm honey to thin out consistency for smoother blending.

Stir honey into balance of ingredients and whip thoroughly with wire whisk or hand mixer.

Store in refrigerator.

Makes a little more than 1 quart.

This mellow combination of flavors is typical of dressings served in Japanese restaurants.

Mitsukoshi Restaurant's Ginger Dressing
Japan Showcase, Epcot Center, Lake Buena Vista

2 good-size pieces fresh
  ginger, about 2 ounces
1 medium to large onion,
  quartered
3 cups vegetable oil
1 cup vinegar
1¾ cups soy sauce
1½ tablespoons tomato paste
¼ lemon
1 medium garlic clove
1¾ cups water

Soak ginger in cold water for a few minutes to make it easier to remove outer skin. Divide ingredients in half and process each half in the work bowl of a food processor fitted with a steel blade. The mixture should have a smooth consistency. Combine both batches and refrigerate.

Makes 2 quarts.

The Outback is located next to the hotel's Laughing Kookaburra Lounge. The restaurant is open nightly and reservations are suggested.

Outback Restaurant's House Dressing
Buena Vista Palace, Lake Buena Vista

2 tablespoons fresh lemon
   juice
4 extra-large eggs
2 tablespoons Dijon mustard
1 pint good-quality light
   vegetable salad oil
$1/2$ teaspoon Worcestershire
   sauce
4 tablespoons red-wine
   vinegar
1 tablespoon chopped fresh
   parsley
1 tablespoon chopped fresh
   garlic
Basil to taste
Oregano to taste
Thyme to taste
Black pepper to taste
Salt to taste

Place all ingredients in the work bowl of a blender and mix well to emulsify. Adjust seasoning to taste. Store in refrigerator.

Makes about $1^1/2$ pints.

Marko's Heritage Inn in Port Orange is a favorite stop along Volusia County's Old Dixie Highway. The family-owned operation serves home-style specialties.

Marko's Seminole French Dressing
Port Orange

1 cup salad oil
1/4 cup lemon juice
1 1/2 cups ketchup
1/2 cup sugar
1/2 cup grated onion
1/3 cup grated horseradish
1/4 cup Worcestershire sauce
1/2 cup apple-cider vinegar

In a small bowl, combine all ingredients and mix well. Refrigerate dressing until ready to use.

Makes about 6 cups.

Recipe note: For more texture, use chopped, not grated, onions.

Straub's Thousand Island Dressing
Altamonte Springs, Orlando

1 quart mayonnaise
10 ounces Major Grey's chutney
½ cup Heinz chili sauce
1 hard-cooked egg, chopped
1 tablespoon plus 1 teaspoon
    finely diced yellow onion
4 teaspoons finely diced red
    pepper

In a medium-size bowl, combine all ingredients in the order listed and blend well.

Store dressing in the refrigerator until ready to use.

Makes about 1½ quarts.

This is a delicious make-ahead lunch salad. Combine all the ingredients and add the mayonnaise at the last minute.

Lunching Pad's Pita Vegetable Mix
Walt Disney World, Lake Buena Vista

$\frac{1}{2}$ cup diced tomato
$\frac{1}{2}$ cup diced cucumber
$\frac{1}{4}$ cup diced zucchini
2 tablespoons finely minced onion
1 medium-size green bell pepper, seeded and diced
1 small carrot, shredded
$\frac{1}{4}$ cup black olive wedges
$\frac{1}{4}$ cup shredded Swiss cheese
$\frac{1}{4}$ cup shredded Cheddar cheese
$\frac{1}{4}$ cup grated Parmesan cheese
1 tablespoon minced fresh garlic
$\frac{1}{2}$ cup mayonnaise (not salad dressing)
4 pita pockets

Blend vegetables and cheeses into mayonnaise.
Stuff mixture into 4 pita pockets.
Makes 4 servings.

Entrees

Sheila Alexander's Vegetarian Chili is a richly flavored hearty menu choice at the Thornton Park Cafe.

Thornton Park Cafe's Vegetarian Chili
Orlando

1 red bell pepper, coarsely
   chopped
2 yellow bell peppers, coarsely
   chopped
1 green bell pepper, coarsely
   chopped
1 onion, coarsely chopped
1 tablespoon minced garlic
1½ tablespoons Inner Beauty
   Hot Sauce (available in
   gourmet stores) or
  ½ tablespoon Tabasco sauce
1½ teaspoons cayenne
   pepper
½ teaspoon thyme
1½ tablespoons oregano
1½ teaspoons cumin
1½ tablespoons chili powder
1 teaspoon salt
¼ teaspoon black pepper
1 (19-ounce) can cannelloni
   beans, undrained
1 (16-ounce) can black beans,
   undrained
1 (16-ounce) can kidney beans,
   undrained
2 (28-ounce) cans whole
   tomatoes, coarsely chopped,
   undrained
2 (28-ounce) cans tomato sauce

Put all ingredients in large saucepan or stockpot, including the liquid from canned beans and tomatoes.

Simmer, stirring occasionally, 20 to 30 minutes or until chili is thickened to desired consistency.

Makes 14 to 16 servings.

Recipe note: This chili freezes well.

Add the hot sauce according to personal taste. The restaurant's version is very spicy.

The Garden Patch is a favorite lunch-hour retreat for those working in downtown Orlando's business hub. The eatery serves a variety of natural foods and vegetarian specialties.

The Garden Patch's Vegetarian Chili
Orlando

1 (36-ounce) can Bush's Best
   Hot Mexican Beans,
   undrained
1 (36-ounce) can kidney beans,
   undrained
1 (30-ounce) can tomato juice
1 (16-ounce) can diced
   tomatoes
1 small onion, chopped
2 green peppers, chopped
1 teaspoon paprika
1 teaspoon oregano
1 teaspoon onion powder
1 teaspoon minced fresh garlic
1 teaspoon sweet basil
2 teaspoons chili powder
1 medium-size wedge Havarti
   cheese, chopped

To make in the microwave, combine all of the ingredients in a microwave-safe casserole dish. Microwave on high (100 percent) power for 45 minutes, rotate and stir halfway through the cooking cycle.

To make on the stovetop, combine all of the ingredients in a large soup kettle or stockpot, simmer for 2 hours, stirring occasionally. Add more liquid if necessary.

Makes about 1 gallon (freezes well).

This dish has noodles sauteed in olive oil with tomatoes and red pepper. It is just one of many Italian specialties offered by proprietors Gregory and Linda Gentile.

Antonio's Pennette All'Arrabbiata
Maitland

2 (1 pound, 12-ounce) cans Italian plum tomatoes

2 to 3 fresh basil leaves, chopped

1 small bunch Italian parsley, chopped, stems discarded

1 teaspoon salt or to taste

3 cloves garlic, chopped, not pressed

1/4 to 1/3 cup 100 percent pure olive oil

2 to 4 pinches crushed red pepper

1 or 2 pinches white pepper

1 1/2 to 2 pounds penne noodles

1 or 2 anchovy fillets, finely chopped

1/2 cup grated fresh Parmigiano-Reggiano cheese (see note)

In large, heavy-bottomed skillet or saucepan, add olive oil. Over low heat, warm olive oil, add garlic and simmer until garlic begins to turn almond. Stir in tomatoes, salt, crushed red pepper, white pepper and anchovies. On medium high heat, cook about 15 to 20 minutes or until tomato liquid is reduced.

While sauce is cooking, in large 6- to 8-quart stock pot or saucepan, bring water with teaspoon of salt to a boil. Add penne noodles and cook for 8 to 9 minutes, depending on your preference.

When sauce has reduced, add chopped Italian parsley and basil, stir, add well-drained pasta, mix well. Top with Parmigiano-Reggiano and garnish with parsley.

Makes 6 servings.

Recipe notes: Parmigiano-Reggiano is Italy's pre-eminent Parmesan cheese. It has a granular texture that melts in the mouth. Parmigiano-Reggianos are often aged 2 years and come from Bologna, Mantua, Modena or Parma Italy. It is available in Italian markets, specialty stores and some supermarkets.

Antonio's Farfalle al Ragu Pollo con Finocchio
Maitland

½ large yellow onion, finely chopped
½ cup extra-virgin olive oil
2 cups cubed boneless, skinless fresh chicken
¼ cup finely chopped fennel bulb
¼ cup anisette liqueur
2 cups chicken stock
¼ cup tomato paste
1 pound dry farfalle (bow tie) pasta
4 quarts water

Saute onion in oil until tender, add chicken pieces. Stir in fennel, anisette and chicken stock. Continue cooking over medium-high heat for about 10 minutes to reduce liquid content. Then add tomato paste very slowly, stirring well with each addition. Simmer 10 minutes. Finished product should be orange, not red. Set aside but keep warm.

In large saucepot, bring 4 quarts water to a boil. Add dry farfelle pasta slowly, stirring constantly. Return to a boil and continue cooking 7 to 9 minutes or until pasta is al dente. Drain well and toss with hot chicken sauce.

Makes 8 servings.

This chicken dish is a favorite of Anthony's regulars. The Orlando restaurant is open for dinner Monday through Saturday and for lunch Tuesday through Friday.

Anthony's Chicken Cacciatoro
Winter Park

4 chicken breast fillets, skinned
Olive oil
$\frac{1}{2}$ large onion, chopped
12 fresh mushrooms, sliced
2 red bell peppers, chopped
1 tablespoon black pepper
1 tablespoon salt or to taste
1 teaspoon oregano
1 (28-ounce) can crushed tomatoes
1 cup chablis
1 cup chicken broth
Pasta of choice

Slice chicken into large pieces.

In small amount of olive oil, saute chicken with onions, mushrooms and red pepper until vegetables are slightly transparent.

Season with salt, pepper and oregano; stir in tomatoes, wine and chicken broth.

Bring to boil, reduce heat and simmer 15 minutes.

Cook pasta of choice while sauce is simmering.

Drain pasta and serve Chicken Cacciatoro over pasta.

Makes 2 to 4 servings depending on size of portions.

The Gables is one of Lake County's best-kept secrets. The restaurant has a lovely garden view and is with in walking distance of Mount Dora's shopping district.

The Gables' Pasta With Shellfish Primavera
Mount Dora

½ cup reduced shrimp stock
  (instructions follow)
2 bay leaves
1 pound tri-color pasta
  noodles or flavored pasta of
  choice
1 pound scallops
1 pound medium shrimp,
  peeled and deveined
½ pound butter
¼ cup chopped shallots
1 tablespoon finely chopped
  garlic
½ cup flour
1 quart heavy cream
1 cup Madeira wine
½ cup grated Parmesan cheese
Salt and black pepper to taste
Chopped fresh dill to taste
3 cups sauteed vegetables of
  choice
Paprika-dusted poached
  shellfish for garnish
  (optional)

To prepare shrimp stock, peel shrimp and brown shells in butter until toasted. Add 1 cup water and 2 bay leaves and reduce in half over high heat. Strain and set stock aside. Cook pasta; set aside.

Saute seafood with shallots and garlic in ½ pound of butter. Add flour and stir briskly until smooth and creamy. Stir in cream and Madeira wine; simmer 20 minutes (stirring frequently) over low to medium heat until bubbles occur and sauce thickens. Add shrimp stock and stir. Add salt, pepper and dill to taste.

Reheat pasta in boiling salted water for 15 seconds; drain. Arrange pasta on plates; smother noodles with sauce mixture and encircle with sauteed vegetables. Sprinkle with Parmesan cheese. Garnish with paprika-dusted poached shellfish if desired.

Makes 4 servings.

This superb saltimbocca alla Romana is sometimes called saltimbocca alla Sorrentina. Christini's specializes in classic Italian cuisine.

Christini's Saltimbocca alla Romana
Orlando

1 pound fresh spinach
$1/2$ stick butter
$1/4$ cup olive oil
$1/4$ cup plus 5 tablespoons all-purpose flour
1 teaspoon sage
1 pound veal, thinly sliced and flattened
$1/4$ cup Marsala wine
1 stick butter
Salt and pepper to taste
2 ounces prosciutto
3 hard-boiled eggs, thinly sliced

Soak spinach in ice water for 10 minutes to remove any dirt or grit that may be on the leaves. Rinse spinach, boil 5 minutes. Drain well. In frying pan, saute spinach in $1/2$ stick butter over medium heat for 5 minutes. In a separate frying pan, heat the olive oil over high heat; be careful to avoid flame-ups.

Mix flour and sage well, flour veal lightly with the mixture and saute in oil on both sides until golden brown. Drain off remaining oil and to the veal in pan add Marsala wine, 1 stick butter, salt and pepper to taste.

Reduce heat to medium and saute both sides of veal. Form a bed of spinach on an oval platter; place veal on spinach and cover with thin slices of prosciutto and 3 to 4 egg slices per piece of veal. Pour remaining pan sauce over dish and serve hot.

Makes 4 servings.

Fresh seafood is the featured attraction at Hemingway's. Terrace diners at the Key West-themed restaurant can enjoy the Hyatt Grand Cypress' lush landscaping.

Hemingway's Mussels With Fettuccine
Hyatt Grand Cypress Resort, Lake Buena Vista

6 mussels
3 ounces fettuccine
½ tablespoon Pesto (recipe follows)
½ tablespoon minced garlic
Splash white wine
1 tablespoon butter
Salt and pepper to taste
Grated Parmesan cheese to taste

Steam mussels until open. Pick from shell and clean. Cook fettuccine briefly until al dente in boiling water to cover. Drain well. In saute pan place pesto, butter and mussels and swirl over heat until butter is melted and of a creamy consistency. Add fettuccine and dash of white wine. Stir and fold until heated through. Add salt and pepper to taste. Sprinkle with Parmesan cheese and serve.

Makes 1 serving.

Pesto

1 bunch fresh basil
1 tablespoon chopped garlic
½ cup olive oil
1 tablespoon grated Parmesan cheese
1 ounce pine nuts

Wash and trim stems from fresh basil. Pat dry. Combine all ingredients in blender or food processor bowl and puree. Unused pesto sauce may be refrigerated or portion-frozen in an ice cube tray.

Makes about 2 cups.

This is just one of nine fresh fish specialties offered nightly at this delightful restaurant. Jerry Moran adapted this recipe for home preparation.

La Cena's Grouper With Mushrooms
Longwood

Flour seasoned to taste with salt and pepper for dredging
1 (10-ounce) thin lean fillet of grouper or any firm, lean fresh fish
2 eggs, well beaten
Bland vegetable oil to fill a skillet 1/8 inch deep
4 or 5 medium size shiitake mushrooms
2 teaspoons butter, divided
1 ounce demiglace (see note) or strong, dark roast beef gravy or drippings
½ ounce chicken or veal stock
Dash lemon juice

Dredge fillet in seasoned flour, dip in well-beaten egg to coat. Gently saute in oil until fish is done and flakes to the touch. Drain or blot well with paper towels. Set aside and reserve.

In second skillet or saucepan, saute shiitake mushrooms in 1 teaspoon butter, when slightly tender (about 30 seconds), stir in demiglace and stock. Reduce volume by one-third by boiling mixture. (This process causes some of the liquid to evaporate, thereby thickening the consistency and intensifying the flavor.)

Add dash lemon juice to accent, adjust seasoning. Just before serving, whisk in 1 teaspoon butter to thicken sauce. Serve over sauteed fillet. Sauce should be prepared quickly so that it is presented fresh.

Makes 1 or 2 servings.

Recipe notes: Demiglace is a rich brown sauce that is used as a base for many other sauces. It is available in some specialty foods stores.

La Cena Ristorante
Italian Continental Cuisine

This colorful chicken presentation has been a popular menu choice since the restaurant opened in 1986. Shop for sour orange juice at Cuban markets.

Pebbles' Chicken With Sour Orange Sauce
Lake Buena Vista, Longwood, Orlando, Winter Park

2 (3- to 4-ounce) skinless, boneless chicken breasts with tenderloins removed
Flour for dredging, seasoned to taste with 2 parts salt to 1 part each white pepper and granulated garlic
2 tablespoons white wine
1 tablespoon sherry
1 tablespoon sour orange juice
3 ounces chicken or veal stock
1 teaspoon chopped garlic
1 teaspoon arrowroot flour
Olive oil for sauteing
1 tablespoon softened butter
2 plum tomatoes cut in wedges
$\frac{1}{4}$ to $\frac{1}{2}$ avocado, sliced

Pound chicken breasts between sheets of wax paper until flattened and thin. Dust well with seasoned flour. Saute in 1 tablespoon olive oil until golden brown. Transfer to preheated 350F oven and bake about 10 minutes. Remove and keep warm while finishing sauce.

In saucepan with $\frac{1}{4}$ teaspoon olive oil, saute garlic. Stir in white wine, sherry, stock and sour orange juice. Blend arrowroot flour in small amount of water, slowly blend into sauce and stir well until smooth. Simmer, stirring as needed, 5 minutes. Season to taste with salt and white pepper. Fold in softened butter. Add tomato wedges, remove when heated through. Pour sauce over chicken breasts on heated platter; garnish with alternating wedges of tomatoes and avocado slices.

Makes 2 servings.

Recipe notes: If you can't find sour orange juice, substitute 2 teaspoons of orange juice mixed with 1 teaspoon of vinegar.

This wonderful veal dish includes prosciutto, peppers and fontina cheese. The cheese is available in most supermarkets and all specialty cheese stores.

Christini's Vitello del Monferrato
Orlando

12 (1½-ounce) medallions of
  veal
Salt and freshly ground black
  pepper
½ cup all-purpose flour
6 ounces clarified butter (1½
  sticks)
6 ounces dry white wine
4 ounces veal stock
8 thin slices imported
  prosciutto ham
3 whole roasted fresh green or
  red peppers, quartered
8 slices fontina or mozzarella
  cheese

Season each veal medallion with salt and pepper to taste; coat lightly with flour. Melt butter in a heavy saute pan and brown veal quickly on both sides. Add white wine and veal stock, simmer 4 minutes. Place one slice of prosciutto on each medallion and cover with one quartered section of roasted pepper. Top with fontina cheese. Place pan in 350F oven just long enough to melt cheese.

Makes 4 servings.

CHRISTINI'S
RISTORANTE ITALIANO

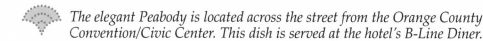

The elegant Peabody is located across the street from the Orange County Convention/Civic Center. This dish is served at the hotel's B-Line Diner.

The Peabody's Crab Cakes and Sauce
Orlando

½ small Spanish onion,
   finely diced
1 small green pepper, finely
   diced
1 small red pepper, finely
   diced
6 sprigs of parsley, finely
   chopped
1 ounce (1 small head) freshly
   chopped garlic
½ cup olive oil
Salt and ground black pepper
   to taste
Cayenne pepper to taste
2 eggs
1 cup dry bread crumbs
½ cup all-purpose flour
6 ounces crab meat
Fine bread crumbs for
   dredging
Vegetable oil for deep-frying

Dipping sauce:
½ cup mayonnaise
2 tablespoons sherry
½ teaspoon cayenne pepper
1 tablespoon lemon juice

Heat olive oil in a skillet; add onion, peppers, parsley, garlic, salt and peppers and saute about 3 minutes. Let cool.

Put mixture in a bowl and using a rubber spatula mix in eggs, dry bread crumbs, flour and crab meat (put crab meat in last to prevent it from breaking too much while mixing with other ingredients). Form crab cakes. Dip each cake in fine bread crumbs and deep-fry at 375F until golden brown.

Mix ingredients listed for dipping sauce, chill in refrigerator. Serve with crab cakes.

Makes 4 servings.

The key to the success of this dish is the use of fresh ingredients – garlic and ginger – in the marinade. The recipe can also be prepared with beef and chicken.

Lutheran Tower's Teriyaki Pork
Orlando

2 cups soy sauce
2 cups water
1 pound brown sugar
¼ cup Burgundy
1 ounce (about 4 cloves) freshly minced garlic
Fresh ginger to taste, peeled, chopped in blender or food processor
3- to 4-pound boneless pork loin
3 tablespoons cornstarch dissolved in cold water for each cup of marinade-glaze desired

Combine soy sauce, water, brown sugar, wine, garlic and ginger in a saucepan. Place pan over medium high heat, bring to boil but do not let liquid boil over. Cook about 10 minutes, stirring, until sugar is dissolved. Pour hot sauce over pork loin and marinate two days in refrigerator. Turn roast in pan once or twice during that time so that meat will be evenly marinated. Remove pork from marinade; reserve liquid. Roast meat about 3 hours at 275F.

To make glaze, place 1 cup of marinade in saucepan and, over medium heat, stir in dissolved cornstarch and continue cooking and stirring until thickened. Brush glaze on pork. If desired, balance of marinade may be thickened and cooked to gravy consistency to serve over rice. Serve with stir-fried fresh vegetables.

Makes 1 quart of marinade.

David Nina, Sea World's executive chef, created this superb entree for the attraction's Polynesian Luau. Mahi-mahi is available at seafood markets.

Sea World's Mahi-Mahi & Pina Colada Sauce
Orlando

4 (6-ounce) mahi-mahi fillets
1/2 cup flour
1 teaspoon seasoned salt
3 whole eggs
1/2 cup liquid margarine
1 tablespoon margarine or
   butter
Pina Colada Sauce (recipe
   follows)
2 tablespoons toasted sliced
   almonds and 1/4 cup toasted
   shredded coconut for
   garnish

Combine flour and salt. Dredge fish in seasoned flour. Beat eggs and put into a shallow dish. Put liquid margarine into another shallow dish. Heat 1 tablespoon margarine or butter in a skillet. Dip fillets in beaten egg and carefully dip in liquid margarine. Brown both sides of fish in skillet. Remove and bake in oven a 350F oven for about 7 or 8 minutes.

Make Pina Colada Sauce as directed below.

To serve, place a pool of sauce on 4 plates. Put prepared fish on the sauce and ribbon additional sauce over top. Liberally sprinkle coconut and almonds over top.

Makes 4 servings.

Pina Colada Sauce

3/4 cup pina colada drink mix
3/4 cup heavy cream
1 tablespoon liquid margarine
1 tablespoon flour

Make a pale roux by stirring flour and margarine together over medium-high heat for 3 or 4 minutes. Combine the pina colada mix and cream. Slowly whisk the mixture into roux. Simmer for 12 to 15 minutes.

This upscale Italian eatery is a favorite of the downtown crowd. In addition to Orlando, Lombardi's restaurants are located in Dallas, Las Vegas, Miami and Phoenix.

Lombardi's Rigatoni al Telefono con Salsiccia
Orlando

½ pound rigatoni (wide tube shaped pasta)
1 tablespoon olive oil
1 cup diced yellow onions
12 ounces fennel bulk sausage (available at Italian stores)
⅓ cup white wine
½ teaspoon fennel seeds
1½ cups diced plum tomatoes, reserve drained juice
1 cup reserved plum tomato juice
½ cup shredded mozzarella cheese
Salt and pepper to taste

Cook pasta until al dente (not soft or overdone). Drain and reserve. In separate pan, saute onions with olive oil until they caramelize; do not burn.

Stir in sausage and saute until done, stirring to break up sausage meat. Drain excess fat from pan. Stir into pan white wine and fennel seeds while still on saute heat, and reduce wine by half. Add tomatoes and tomato juice. Stir well and bring to a simmer. Cook until desired consistency is achieved. Add mozzarella and pasta to pan. Mix well before serving.

Makes 2 servings.

Sleepy Hollow Tea Room's rich custard is a winning choice for brunch or lunch. Serve it with a fresh fruit salad.

Sleepy Hollow's Broccoli Quiche
Orlando

2 cups fresh broccoli, chopped or broken into florets
1 (9-inch) unbaked deep-dish pie shell
10 ounces sharp Cheddar cheese
1/8 cup diced onion
1 teaspoon chopped chives
1 (12-ounce) can evaporated milk
3 eggs
1/2 teaspoon salt
1/4 teaspoon pepper
1/4 teaspoon granulated garlic
1 teaspoon lemon juice

Preheat oven to 350F.

Wash broccoli and chop or break into florets (frozen broccoli, thawed, may be substituted). Place in bottom of pie shell, sprinkle with cheese. Mix balance of ingredients and pour onto broccoli and cheese. Bake in preheated oven about 45 minutes or until custard tests done.

Serve in wedges.

Makes 8 servings.

Recipe notes: If using a frozen ready-made crust, use the deep-dish size.

Chef Louis Perotte has created a four-serving version of this salmon dish for home preparation.

Le Coq au Vin's Salmon and Champagne Sauce
Orlando

2 shallots, finely diced
1/2 cup champagne or white wine
2 tablespoons champagne vinegar (available in some supermarkets and gourmet shops)
1 stick unsalted butter cut in small pieces
2/3 cup heavy cream
Salt and freshly ground pepper to taste
4 (5-ounce) skinless salmon fillets

To make sauce, combine champagne or wine, shallots and vinegar in small saucepan. On medium heat, bring to a boil and reduce until almost dry (no more than 1 tablespoon of liquid left). Add cream and bring to a boil, reduce until cream looks thick and almost buttery. Lower heat and add butter, a piece at a time, whisking constantly until all butter has been added and blended in. Do not boil. Remove from heat and season to taste. Keep warm until ready to serve. Season salmon lightly with salt and pepper. Butter bottom of a baking dish large enough to hold the fish with a little space between pieces.

Place salmon in dish, pour some water (about 1/3 cup) in dish, cover tightly with aluminum foil and bake in 350F oven until done, about 10 minutes depending on thickness. Remove salmon fillets onto warm plates. Pour remaining pan juices into sauce, stir and spoon sauce over warm salmon.

Makes 4 servings.

Recipe notes: This sauce would be excellent served with chicken.

Chicken Amandine is a popular menu choice at the Citrus Club in downtown Orlando. Calorie-counters can omit the sauce and top the chicken with a squeeze of fresh lemon or lime juice.

Citrus Club's Chicken Amandine
Orlando

4 (5-ounce) boneless, skinless chicken breasts
½ cup flour seasoned with salt, pepper and garlic powder
2 eggs
¼ cup milk
4 ounces dry bread crumbs
4 ounces sliced almonds, toasted and partially crushed
Vegetable oil to coat saute skillet

White wine sauce:
¼ cup vegetable oil
⅓ cup flour
½ cup dry white wine
½ cup chicken stock
¼ large onion, chopped
1 bay leaf
Pinch of thyme
½ cup heavy cream
¼ stick butter
8 sprigs of chives, chopped
Salt and pepper to taste

To make sauce combine flour and oil in a shallow pan, blend well. Cook over medium heat 4 to 6 minutes, stirring continually, to make a roux. Do not allow to brown. Remove from heat and reserve in cool place.

Combine wine, stock and onion in saucepan. Over high heat, reduce liquid by half. Stir cooled roux into reduced stock, stirring vigorously with wire whip. When well-blended, add bay leaf, thyme, salt and pepper. Cook 20 minutes over medium heat, stirring constantly.

Stir in heavy cream and simmer 10 more minutes. Remove from heat and strain through a fine sieve. Whisk in butter and chives and adjust seasoning to taste.

Dredge chicken breasts in seasoned flour. Shake off excess. Lightly beat eggs and milk; dip floured chicken in egg-milk mixture. Combine crumbs and almond slices; dredge chicken in mixture and press to make coating adhere. Brown chicken on both sides in oil.

Place breasts on lightly-oiled cookie sheet in a 350F oven and bake 15 to 20 minutes until tender and moist. Serve with wine sauce.

Enzo's Restaurant on the Lake is located in a beautifully restored old-Florida home. It is tucked among the trees at 1130 N. U.S. Highway 17-92 in Longwood.

Enzo's Penne a la Vodka
Longwood

16 ounces dry penne pasta, cooked according to package directions (see note)
1 medium onion, finely chopped
2 tablespoons butter
2 tablespoons olive oil
1 (28-ounce) can Italian plum tomatoes, shredded or pureed
8 ounces heavy whipping cream
Pepper vodka (see note)
Pinch salt to taste
Grated Parmesan cheese

Saute onions in butter and olive oil until transparent. Add shredded or pureed tomatoes with juice. Cook over medium heat 20 to 25 minutes or until all liquid content is reduced. In separate saucepan, cook pasta according to package directions, drain well and set aside.

When tomato sauce is ready, stir in heavy cream. Bring to a near boil, reduce heat and cook 2 to 3 minutes until cream and tomatoes are well blended. Stir in pepper vodka, mix well. Stir in hot cooked penne pasta and salt. Stir together to blend. Liberally sprinkle with grated Parmesan.

Makes 4 servings.

Recipe notes: Pepper vodka is a commercial item available at many liquor stores, but it does not have the concentrated flavor Enzo Perlini prefers. For a homemade version, stir $1/4$ teaspoon red crushed pepper in 4 tablespoons of vodka. Put aside and let marinate 3 hours or overnight. Use a coffee filter or fine cloth napkin to filter peppered vodka. Remove and discard filter and set vodka concentrate aside.

Penne is large straight tubes of macaroni cut on the diagonal.

This recipe was created by Craig Spurza for the Marriott's corporate recipe contest.

Garden Terrace's Lasagna Roulades
Orlando Marriott World Center

1 medium-size onion, chopped
1 (10-ounce) package spinach, thawed
2 pounds chicken breast meat or tenders
Butter or olive oil for sauteing
1 pound mushrooms, sliced
2 pounds ricotta cheese
1 pound Parmesan cheese, grated
½ pound lasagna noodles
Salt and pepper to taste

Drain thawed spinach in a colander until completely dry. Cook lasagna noodles according to package directions. Preheat oven to 350F.

Saute chopped onion, spinach, chicken and mushrooms in butter or olive oil until chicken is cooked through.

Put onion and chicken mixture in the work bowl of a food processor and coarsely chop. Mix in the cheeses and salt and pepper. Lay out cooked pasta on a work surface. Spread onion and chicken mixture over noodles and roll up. Bake lasagna rolls in oven for 10 to minutes.

Makes 4 servings.

Recipe notes: Depending on how generous you are with the filling, you may have some left over. This filling can also be wrapped in phyllo dough or puff pastry and baked until phyllo or puff pastry is golden brown.

Chicken tenders are strips of white meat that are sold in the meat department of most supermarkets. They can also be used in stir-fry recipes.

Sun Coast Restaurant's Chicken Pot Pie
Orlando

2 pounds cooked chicken, white and dark meat, diced
$^1/_2$ cup green peas, thawed
$^1/_4$ to $^1/_2$ cup sliced cooked carrots
1 medium onion, chopped
2 to 3 ribs celery, chopped
1 tablespoon butter
3 ounces chicken base (see note)
3 cups boiling water
8 tablespoons butter or margarine, divided
$^3/_4$ cup flour (for stiff roux)
3 cups biscuit mix

Heat oven to 350F.

Saute onions and celery in 1 tablespoon butter; set aside. Blend chicken base into boiling water. Melt remaining butter over medium-low heat. Blend in flour, and continue cooking, stirring, until roux bubbles. Whisk in chicken-flavored boiling water. When roux is incorporated, bring to a slow boil. Reduce heat and continue whisking until sauce thickens, 5 minutes. Stir in chicken and vegetables; set aside.

Make biscuit mix following package directions. Roll out enough dough to cover 6 individual casseroles. Spoon chicken mixture into baking dishes. Cover each with dough. Crimp edges and pierce dough with a fork. Bake 45 minutes to 1 hour or until crust is golden.

Makes 6 servings.

Recipe notes: Three cups boiling chicken broth, or 4 bouillon cubes dissolved in 3 cups boiling water can be substituted for chicken base. In testing, Bisquick batter was too soft to roll so we dropped the dough on the chicken mixture and smoothed it over, sealing at the edges.

If using glass pans, reduce heat to 325F.

Buster Silva's dish is a breeze to duplicate in the home kitchen. Keep a supply of Scampi Butter stashed in the freezer for the next time you want to make this dish.

Lido's Shrimp Scampi
Orlando

2 tablespoons sherry
7 large shrimp, shelled and
  deveined
Scampi Butter (recipe follows)

Spoon sherry into a single-serving casserole dish or ramekin. Line casserole dish with prepared shrimp. Top liberally with Scampi Butter (at least 1 tablespoon).

Place in a preheated 400F oven and bake for about 10 minutes or until shrimp are tender.

Makes 1 serving.

Scampi Butter

1 pound butter
¼ cup olive oil
3 to 4 tablespoons minced
  garlic
¼ cup chopped parsley
Juice of 1 lemon

Soften butter. Blend with remaining ingredients. Whip at high speed until mixture is light and creamy. It will appear to be almost white when it is the right consistency.

Refrigerate until firm. Use to taste in Shrimp Scampi recipe.

To store remaining flavored butter, wrap tightly and freeze.

Makes 1 pound.

This is a unique eggplant-seafood creation with a snappy Cajun hollandaise dressing. It takes a bit of work to prepare, but it makes a sumptuous presentation.

Le Coq au Vin's Eggplant Bayou Teche
Orlando

3 medium eggplants, halved
    lengthwise and peeled
Salt and pepper to taste
Seasoned flour for dredging
2 eggs beaten with
    2 tablespoons milk
Seasoned bread crumbs for
    dredging
Oil for frying
1/2 pound lump crab meat,
    picked over
30 cooked and peeled medium
    shrimp
Cajun hollandaise (see note)

Cut a thin slice off the rounded side of each eggplant half so it will sit level. Carve out the center to hold crab meat and shrimp. Sprinkle each eggplant with salt and pepper, dredge in seasoned flour, coat with a milk and egg wash, then dredge in seasoned bread crumbs.

Fry halves in hot oil until golden brown; drain on paper towels. While still warm, place an equal amount of crab meat in the centers and top each with five shrimp. To serve, place eggplant in warm oven for about 5 minutes to heat crab meat and shrimp. Place on warm plate and top with Cajun Hollandaise.

Makes 6 servings.

Recipe notes: To make hollandaise, melt 1 pound of butter over low heat. Increase heat and bring butter to a rapid boil. Remove from heat and cool for 3 minutes. Skim foam from top. In a blender at medium speed, combine 4 egg yolks, 2 teaspoons lemon juice, 1/2 teaspoon Worcestershire sauce and 2 teaspoons warm water. Add butter gradually into egg mixture. Make sure butter added is well mixed into sauce before adding more. Keep sauce warm until ready to serve.

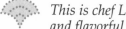 *This is chef Louis Perotte's super signature dish. Chicken in wine is a succulent and flavorful entree for any occasion.*

Le Coq au Vin's Chicken in Red Wine
Orlando

2 (1½ - to 2-pound) chickens, quartered and deboned
1 carrot, diced
1 medium onion, diced
1 clove garlic, chopped
2½ cups Burgundy red wine
2 fresh tomatoes, quartered
1 bay leaf
1 teaspoon thyme
3 tablespoons vegetable oil
3 cups chicken stock
6 ounces mushrooms, quartered
2 ounces thick-sliced smoked bacon, cut in ¼-inch pieces
12 pearl onions, peeled and cooked
Salt and pepper to taste
Flour for dredging

Cut chicken wings off at second joint. Season all pieces with salt and pepper and dredge lightly in flour. Put oil in a skillet. When oil is hot, brown chicken on both sides. Remove chicken and set aside on paper towels to drain. Discard oil in skillet.

In same skillet, toss carrots, onions and garlic for 2 minutes on medium heat, stirring to prevent sticking. Deglaze pan with wine. Add tomatoes, bay leaf and thyme. Bring to a boil and reduce by half.

Put chicken legs in a pot. Add stock and wine stock. Simmer for 20 minutes over medium-low heat. Add remaining chicken. Simmer 15 minutes. Remove chicken from pan; keep warm. Reduce cooking stock by ⅓ and strain through a sieve, pressing hard with a spatula to extract as much liquid as possible. Pour sauce over chicken. In a small skillet, brown bacon. Discard drippings and saute mushrooms, onions and bacon on medium-high heat for 2 minutes. Add sauteed vegetables and bacon to chicken. Stir gently. For optimum flavor, keep dish covered and warm for 30 minutes before serving.

Makes 4 servings.

This sprawling Lake County resort is a popular location for corporate retreats, wedding receptions, banquets and Sunday brunch.

Mission Inn's Chicken Florentine
Howey-in-the-Hills

4 (5-ounce) boneless, skinless
   chicken breasts
¼ cup seasoned flour
¼ cup olive oil
1 small white onion, thinly
   sliced
1 teaspoon chopped shallots
½ teaspoon chopped garlic
¼ cup chopped fresh
   mushrooms
1 tablespoon butter
1 package fresh spinach,
   stemmed and cleaned
½ cup Chablis wine
¼ pound grated Monterey
   Jack cheese for garnish

Sauce:
1 quart hot chicken stock
1 stick butter
½ cup flour
¼ teaspoon nutmeg
1 (8-ounce) package frozen
   chopped spinach, thawed
   and reserved (do not drain)

Pound out chicken to even thickness between sheets of wax paper. Dust with seasoned flour. Saute both of sides of chicken in olive oil until lightly browned. Remove from pan; set aside. In the same pan, saute onions, shallots, garlic and mushrooms. Stir in butter and cook 30 seconds over high heat. Add spinach and wine. Cook 1 minute and cover; set aside.

To make the sauce, melt 1 stick of butter and stir in ½ cup of flour to make a roux. When smooth, cook 10 minutes over medium heat, stirring occasionally; do not brown. Over medium heat, slowly add stock, blending well to prevent lumps. Add nutmeg and let mixture cook for 10 minutes. Stir in thawed spinach and liquid. Adjust seasoning with salt and pepper to taste and cook 5 minutes.

In an oven-proof casserole, dish layer sauteed fresh spinach mixture, top with chicken breasts. Cover with sauce and sprinkle with grated Monterey Jack cheese.

Bake, uncovered, in 350F oven for 6 minutes. Serve with steamed vegetables and pasta of choice.

Makes 4 servings.

Rob Straub uses only the finest New England sea scallops for this recipe. At the restaurant, the scallops can be ordered broiled or baked.

Straub's New England Sea Scallops
Altamonte Springs, Orlando

9 ounces prime-quality fresh (30 to 40 count) large New England scallops
2 tablespoons seasoned butter
2 tablespoons bread crumbs

Seasoned butter:
4 sticks butter
½ teaspoon salt
1 teaspoon white pepper
5 tablespoons garlic powder

To make seasoned butter, mash and blend seasonings into softened butter. Place on sheet of waxed paper and form into roll. Refrigerate roll. Seasoned butter will keep well in the refrigerator.

Use 2 tablespoons as directed in instructions that follow.

Use remaining roll to season steamed vegetables, cooked seafood or broiled beef.

Arrange sea scallops in individual oven-proof ramekin (baking dish must have sides to retain butter sauce). Dot with 2 room-temperature tablespoons of seasoned butter. Sprinkle with bread crumbs.

Place in preheated 375F oven and bake about 15 minutes or until tender.

Serve immediately.

Makes 1 serving.

The Baby Nova has changed hands many times. This popular entree was developed by chef Arch Maynard.

Baby Nova's Capellini
Winter Park

3 ounces virgin olive oil

4 ripe, fresh tomatoes, 2 thinly sliced, 2 diced

2 teaspoons finely chopped shallots

1 teaspoon finely chopped garlic

2 teaspoons chopped fresh basil

1 teaspoon chopped fresh oregano

Salt and pepper to taste

4 ounces dry white wine

4 ounces tomato puree

1 pound good quality dry capellini (angel hair pasta)

Heat oil in large saucepan.

Add tomatoes, shallots, garlic, basil, oregano, salt and pepper. Saute about $1^1/_2$ minutes. Stir in white wine and tomato puree, simmer 2 minutes. Cook angel hair pasta following package directions. Add to sauce, stir and serve.

Makes 4 to 6 servings.

Serve this brunch or lunch treat with a fresh fruit salad and zucchini muffins.

The Gables' Broccoli Quiche
Mount Dora

1¼ cups shredded Swiss cheese

1¼ cups shredded Cheddar cheese

2 cups broccoli florets, minced

1 (10-inch) prepared pie shell, unbaked

5 eggs, beaten

2 cups half-and-half

½ teaspoon salt

¼ teaspoon ground white pepper

¼ teaspoon ground nutmeg

Preheat oven to 350F.

Combine minced broccoli and shredded Swiss and Cheddar cheeses. Put cheese mixture into prepared pie shell.

Combine remaining ingredients and pour over broccoli-cheese mixture; be careful the custard does not overflow pan.

Bake quiche for 45 to 50 minutes or until firm.

Allow to stand 15 minutes before cutting.

Makes 6 servings.

This creamy seafood casserole is no longer on Park Plaza Gardens' menu. It was created by former executive chef Patrick Reilly.

Park Plaza Gardens' Seafood Homardine
Winter Park

1 cup dry vermouth
1 cup fish stock
2 cups heavy cream
3 shallots, finely diced
1 teaspoon chopped fresh basil
Lemon juice to taste
Salt and freshly ground
   pepper to taste
$\frac{1}{2}$ clove garlic, finely
   chopped
2 ounces button mushrooms,
   quartered
8 medium shrimp
4 medium to large scallops,
   halved
4 ounces lobster meat
16 ounces white fish (snapper,
   grouper, swordfish,
   flounder), cut in bite-size
   pieces
4 lobster claws for garnish
   (optional)
4 tablespoons favorite-recipe
   hollandaise sauce

Bring all liquids except lemon juice to a boil, add shallots, basil, lemon juice, salt and pepper to taste. Remove from heat and let stand 5 minutes for flavors to infuse. Add garlic and mushrooms. Add, in order, shrimp, white fish, scallops, lobster, lobster claws. Cook over medium heat about 3$\frac{1}{2}$ minutes.

Remove lobster claws and reserve, remove seafood and place in bottom of a casserole dish.

Bring liquid left in pan to a boil and reduce by half. Strain over seafood in casserole.

Top with hollandaise. Place under broiler to glaze.

Garnish servings with lobster claws.

Makes 4 servings.

This eatery is a Winter Park favorite. The recipe gets its nice tomato flavor from sun-dried tomatoes.

Bravissimo's Shrimp and Scallops
Winter Park

1 tablespoon butter
1 tablespoon chopped fresh
   garlic
7 to 8 (20 to 30 count) sea
   scallops
2 tablespoons chardonnay
1 tablespoon chopped fresh
   parsley
Salt and pepper to taste
5 to 6 sun-dried tomatoes,
   julienned
4 jumbo shrimp
$1/3$ cup heavy cream, or more
   as desired

In saucepan over medium heat, melt butter; stir in chopped garlic and saute briefly until garlic begins to pale.

Stir in scallops, parsley, salt and pepper, tomatoes and wine. Saute 3 to 4 minutes, stirring, until scallops are tender and wine reduced.

Add shrimp and heavy cream, continue cooking $1^{1}/_{2}$ to $2^{1}/_{2}$ minutes or until shrimp are pink and cream begins to thicken. Add more cream if desired.

Serve over cooked flat noodles of choice.

Makes 1 serving.

This recipe makes butter-tender steaks in a delightful sauce. Sheffields' offers an extensive menu with an emphasis on veal, fresh seafood and aged beef.

Sheffields' Steak Diane
Orlando

1 pound filet mignon sliced
   into 4 medallions or
   4 (4-ounce) beef tenderloins
1 teaspoon butter
2 green onions, chopped
½ teaspoon chopped fresh
   garlic
10 medium mushrooms, sliced
1 ounce Burgundy wine
1 ounce brandy
1 teaspoon Worcestershire
1¼ cup demiglace

Heat skillet on medium, add butter, briefly sear filets on both sides. Drain excess butter, add green onions and garlic and saute only until partially transparent.

Stir in mushrooms and saute, again only until partially tender. Add Burgundy and brandy at the same time, allow to flambe. Add Worcestershire and demiglace; stir, moving meat around skillet.

Simmer until filets are cooked to desired doneness. Place some sauce on two warm plates, place two filets each over sauce, spoon balance of sauce over meat.

Makes 2 servings.

Recipe notes: Demiglace is rich brown sauce. It is available in well-stocked gourmet shops. Many all-purpose cookbooks, such as *Joy of Cooking*, have recipes for making demiglace from scratch.

This fried fish recipe uses an Asian breading rather than the traditional cornmeal coating.

Charlie's Lobster House's Pan Fried Grouper
Winter Park

1 (8-ounce) fresh grouper fillet
Salt and white pepper to taste
Flour for dredging
1 egg, lightly beaten with
    1 tablespoon milk for egg
    wash
Panko Bread Crumbs (see
    note)
3 tablespoons butter

Season grouper with salt and white pepper to taste, dip lightly in flour, then in egg wash. Shake off excess and dredge in Panko breading.

Over low heat, melt butter in saute pan, add grouper fillet and slowly pan fry on both sides until fillet is golden and flakes at the touch of a fork, about 8 to 10 minutes per 1-inch thickness.

Makes 1 serving

Recipe notes: Panko Bread Crumbs are available in Asian grocery stores.

Food, service and atmosphere are top of the line at Epcot's Marrakesh. The couscous called for in this recipe is available in supermarkets and health food stores.

Restaurant Marrakesh's Lamb Couscous
Moroccan Showcase, Epcot Center, Lake Buena Vista

2 gallons water
3½ pounds lamb, cubed
4 to 5 medium onions, chopped
¼ cup olive oil
2 tablespoons salt
1 tablespoon white pepper
½ teaspoon saffron
½ teaspoon yellow food coloring
10 to 12 carrots, peeled and trimmed
2 large turnips, peeled and trimmed
½ small head cabbage, trimmed and cored
3 medium zucchini, trimmed
1 medium eggplant, trimmed
3 medium tomatoes, quartered
½ cup cooked chick peas (garbanzos)
2 tablespoons raisins
2 pounds couscous

In a large kettle, bring 2 gallons of water to rolling boil; add lamb, onions, oil, salt, pepper, saffron and yellow food coloring. Cook 1 hour.

Cut carrots, turnips, cabbage, zucchini and eggplant into thick, 2-inch strips, add to lamb mixture and continue cooking 30 minutes or until vegetables are tender. Add tomatoes and chick peas, cook another 3 minutes.

Cook couscous according to package directions. To serve, place couscous on plate and cover with lamb and vegetable mixture and cooking liquid. Sprinkle with raisins.

Makes 10 servings.

This is a simple, flavorful Italian classic. It takes only a few minutes of preparation time before it's ready to serve and enjoy.

Enzo's Spaghetti alla Carbonara
Longwood

4 ounces spaghetti
½ cup olive oil
2 large tablespoons coarsely
  chopped onion
2 strips bacon, cut into 1-inch
  lengths
1 teaspoon black pepper
1 egg yolk, lightly beaten
¼ cup Romano and Parmesan
  cheese mixture

In a skillet, saute onion in olive oil until translucent. Add bacon and cook until crisp. Stir in black pepper.

Cook spaghetti according to package directions.

Drain spaghetti thoroughly and add to skillet. Toss well over high heat. Add beaten egg yolk and cheese and continue tossing for 2 minutes. Serve hot.

Makes 1 serving.

Enzo's
Restaurant
on the Lake

Almost any Chinese menu includes a lemon-flavored chicken dish. It is best if prepared just before serving.

Orient IV's Lemon Chicken
Lake Mary

2 large skinned and deboned
   chicken breasts
2 ounces rice noodles
8 cups peanut oil

Marinade:
½ teaspoon salt
½ teaspoon sherry
1 tablespoon cornstarch
1 tablespoon cold water
1 egg yolk, beaten
½ teaspoon pepper

Batter:
3 tablespoons cornstarch
9 tablespoons flour
1 tablespoon peanut oil
½ tablespoon baking powder
½ tablespoon salt
1 whole egg
½ teaspoon vinegar
9 tablespoons of ice water

Lemon sauce:
4 tablespoons freshly
   squeezed lemon juice
8 tablespoons water
5 tablespoons sugar
1½ tablespoons cornstarch

Deep-fry rice noodles in 375F oil for about 1 minute; drain on paper towel.

Mix marinade ingredients. Slice each chicken breast in half lengthwise. Put in bowl, add marinade and toss. Let sit for 10 minutes.

Combine ingredients for egg batter and stir well. In a small saucepan, mix lemon sauce ingredients and place over medium heat, stirring constantly, until boiling point is reached. Reduce heat to very low and mixture will congeal.

Reheat oil to deep-fry chicken. Dip each piece of chicken in batter with both hands (1 piece at a time) and let excess batter drip until chicken is lightly coated. Deep-fry until golden brown. Continue process until each piece of chicken is done. Reheat oil until very hot and fry all 4 slices again for about 15 seconds. Drain and slice each piece of chicken into 3 equal pieces; place chicken on a platter on top of the fried noodles.

Warm lemon sauce and pour liberally over chicken. If desired, garnish platter with lemon slices. Serve immediately.

Makes 2 servings.

Cooking food in parchment paper gently steams it done without added fat. Parchment paper can be purchased in some supermarkets and all gourmet stores.

Townsend's Fishhouse's Grouper en Papillote
Orlando

6 (6-ounce) grouper fillets
¼ cup diced fresh broccoli
¼ cup diced fresh carrots
¼ cup diced fresh zucchini
2¼ cups Mushroom Cream
  Sauce (recipe follows)
6 sheets parchment paper,
  about 16 inches by 24 inches
Vegetable oil

Cut 6 large hearts from paper. Brush tops with oil. Divide vegetables into 6 portions, put some of each on the left side of each heart near the center. Put a fillet on top. Ladle 3 ounces of Mushroom Cream Sauce over each. Fold the right half of the paper over the left and, beginning at the top of the heart, seal the pouch by folding up the edge and creasing it tightly. Continue folding around the edge, overlapping each crease. When end is reached a tail will have been created; twist and fold it under the pouch. Bake 10 to 15 minutes at 400F until pouches swell and brown. To serve, cut a cross in the top of each and roll back paper.

Makes 6 servings.

Mushroom Cream Sauce

5 tablespoons butter, divided
4 tablespoons flour
¼ pound sliced mushrooms
2 tablespoons clam base
Pinch chives
Pinch of white pepper
3 large shallots, diced finely
1½ ounces white wine
1 pint heavy cream

In a saucepan, combine 3 tablespoons butter and the flour. Slowly stir in heavy cream. Whip until smooth. Saute diced shallots in remaining butter. Add mushrooms and saute 3 more minutes. Combine cream base with shallots and mushrooms, stir in clam base, white pepper and wine. Simmer 10 minutes, remove from heat and stir in chives.

127

This is a glorious dish that requires concentration in the preparation. The final result is well worth the effort.

Arthur's 27's Snapper With Key Lime Butter
Buena Vista Palace, Lake Buena Vista

6 (4- to 5-ounce) skinned
 snapper fillets
1 cup chopped fresh herbs
 (combination of basil, dill,
 oregano, thyme and parsley)
3 whole eggs, beaten
Flour
Salt and pepper to taste
Olive oil
12 orange sections
30 whole pecans, shelled and
 sauteed

Key lime butter:
1 pound unsalted butter,
 softened
Juice of 3 key limes
3 ounces white wine
Pinch cayenne pepper
1 tablespoon chopped fresh
 parsley
1 ounce demiglace

Whip butter until it doubles in volume. Blend in lime juice, slowly add wine. Season with cayenne pepper and parsley. Finish with demiglace.

On parchment paper, roll out butter about the thickness of a half dollar. Refrigerate.

Lightly dredge snapper fillets in flour, place in beaten egg, remove and sprinkle with chopped herbs, salt and pepper. Set aside for five minutes.

Cover bottom of skillet with small amount of olive oil and brown fish fillets well. Remove from pan, place on baking sheet and finish in 350F oven, about 5 minutes or until fish flakes when tested.

Arrange fish on six plates, place equal number of sauteed pecans around fish. Cut key lime butter into medallions and place one on top of each serving of hot fish. Garnish with fresh orange sections and vegetable of choice.

Makes 6 servings.

Maison & Jardin's elegant garden setting makes it an ideal location for parties and weddings. Chef-owner Bill Bueret is responsible for the fabulous menu.

Maison & Jardin's Veal Chop Alaska
Altamonte Springs

6 (10- to 12-ounce) veal chops
Salt and pepper to taste
Flour
½ cup clarified butter
12 ounces Mushroom Sauce
  (recipe follows)
6 (3½-ounce) slices favorite
  crab meat stuffing or frozen
  crab meat stuffing, thawed
6 slices Havarti cheese, halved
6 scored, cooked mushrooms
  and truffle slices for garnish

Season chops with salt and pepper, dust with flour and brown on both sides in hot clarified butter.

Place chops in a 400F oven and bake about 15 minutes or until tender. Cover 6 oven-proof plates with Mushroom Sauce. Put a chop on each plate, top with crab mixture and cheese strips. Glaze under oven broiler about 30 seconds or until cheese is melted. Center mushroom and truffle garnish on cheese and serve.

Makes 6 servings.

Mushroom Sauce

10 ounces mushrooms, sliced
3 tablespoons butter
2 tablespoons chopped
  shallots
2 ounces brandy
½ cup white wine
1 quart heavy whipping cream
1 tablespoon Knorr demiglace
1 tablespoon flour mixed with
  1 tablespoon melted butter
Salt and pepper

Saute mushrooms in butter until tender. Add shallots and brandy, then carefully flambe. When flame dies, add wine and bring to boil, add cream and return to boil.

Stir in demiglace and flour and butter mixture. Continue cooking 15 minutes to reduce sauce. Season to taste with salt and pepper.

Makes about 1 quart.

This recipe was developed by Ben Barnwell. Barney's Steak and Seafood is a longtime Orlando landmark.

Barney's Shrimp Flamingo
Orlando

14 large (18-count) shrimp
Flour
1 stick butter at room
    temperature
3 tablespoons all-purpose
    flour
$\frac{1}{4}$ teaspoon salt
$\frac{1}{4}$ teaspoon pepper
$\frac{1}{3}$ tablespoon garlic powder
$\frac{3}{4}$ tablespoon chopped chives

Wine sauce:
$1\frac{5}{8}$ ounces dry sherry
$\frac{2}{3}$ ounce wine vinegar
1 ounce water

To make wine sauce, combine dry sherry, wine vinegar and water. Stir to mix and set aside.

Peel and clean shrimp, leaving tails on. Devein and butterfly, wash and towel dry. Dip shrimp in flour to lightly coat and place in baking dish.

Mix butter with the 3 tablespoons flour, salt, pepper, garlic powder and chives. Pour this butter mixture into baking dish. Take each shrimp by the tail and move it around in butter mixture until it is well coated.

Place shrimp in a 475F oven until butter just begins to bubble. Watch carefully so that shrimp do not overcook.

Remove from oven and while still bubbling, distribute wine sauce around baking dish. Using a spoon, stir quickly and well to thicken. Toss shrimp to paint them in the sauce.

Serve immediately.

Makes 2 servings.

This simple chicken presentation makes good use of pantry-ready ingredients. It is a favorite of regulars at the Rolling Hills Golf Club.

Rolling Hills' Bourbon Pecan Chicken
Longwood

2 boneless, skinless chicken breasts
Seasoned flour for dredging
2 tablespoons vegetable oil
1 clove garlic, chopped
3 ounces bourbon
3 tablespoons coarsely chopped pecans
2 ounces honey
3 ounces heavy cream
1/2 stick unsalted butter, well-chilled

Dredge chicken breasts in seasoned flour, shake off excess. Add vegetable oil to skillet and heat; add chicken breasts and saute until golden brown on both sides. Remove and place in oven-safe dish, bake in preheated 350F oven for 5 minutes.

In same skillet, saute garlic for 10 seconds. Stir in bourbon, honey, pecans and heavy cream. Simmer 2 minutes. Remove from heat and gently whisk in cold butter. Season to taste with salt and pepper.

Spoon bourbon sauce over chicken breasts.

Makes 2 servings.

These spicy Maryland-style crab cakes are restaurateur Al Steigerwald's signature menu item at Charlie's Lobster House. Executive chef Wendell Thompson broke down the recipe to home-kitchen proportions.

Charlie's Lobster House's Blue Crab Cakes
Winter Park

3 pounds jumbo lump blue
    crab meat
1¼ cups mayonnaise
3 whole eggs
2 tablespoons dry mustard
1 tablespoon Lea & Perrin's
    Worcestershire sauce
¾ cup diced pimentos
1 cup diced green bell pepper
1¼ cups unseasoned bread
    crumbs

Pick over crab for shells; set aside. In a large bowl, whisk together mayonnaise, eggs, mustard and Worcestershire. Blend into dressing all ingredients except bread crumbs. Fold in crumbs. Shape crab mixture into 4-ounce cakes. Place on baking sheet. Bake in a 425F oven until golden, about 8 to 10 minutes.

Serve 2 cakes per person accompanied on the side with a honey mustard dressing or sauce of choice.

Makes 8 servings.

CHARLIE'S
LOBSTER HOUSE

The Lakeside Inn is a turn-of-the-century country resort with a striking view of Lake Dora.

Lakeside Inn's Chicken Cordon Bleu
Mount Dora

1 (6- to 8-ounce) skinless,
  boneless chicken breast
1 (1-ounce) slice Swiss cheese
1 (1-ounce) slice smoked ham
1 whole egg, beaten
Equal portions of flour and
  bread crumbs for dredging
2 egg whites, beaten until
  peaks form
1½ ounces half-and-half

Place chicken breast between sheets of waxed paper and pound to flatten. Layer breast with 1 slice each Swiss cheese and smoked ham.

Roll chicken breast to enclose cheese and ham; secure with picks if needed. Dip into beaten egg, dredge in flour-bread crumb mixture, shake off excess.

Heat oven to 350F. Place chicken roll on lightly greased baking sheet and bake about 15 minutes or until tender. Remove from oven. Fold half-and-half into stiffly beaten egg whites and garnish chicken with a diagonal strip of the egg white sauce.

Makes 1 serving.

This macaroni dish takes just 10 minutes of cooking time. Only a few ingredients are needed to create this masterpiece.

Enzo's Bucatini
Longwood

4 ounces pasta
2 tablespoons olive oil
2 ounces bacon
2 large pinches black pepper
1 ounce prosciutto
1 tablespoon peas
1 tablespoon sliced fresh
   mushrooms
1½ ounces grated mixed
   Parmesan and Romano
   cheese

Cook pasta 9 to 10 minutes in salted water according to package instructions. Five minutes before pasta is cooked, begin preparing sauce.

Saute bacon with olive oil in skillet until it begins to crisp. Add black pepper and allow to stand for 1 minute. Add prosciutto, stir over heat for 1 minute. Add mushrooms and continue sauteing and stirring for 1 minute. Add peas. Cook for 2 minutes, allowing peas to absorb flavors of the dish. Add cooked, drained pasta and toss gently. Add cheeses and toss again gently.

Serve hot.

Makes 1 serving.

Townsend's Plantation is a beautifully restored home in Orange County. In addition to a full-service restaurant, the Plantation has several rooms available for private dinner parties.

Townsend's Plantation's Mahi-Mahi Amondine
Apopka

4 (8-ounce) mahi-mahi fillets
Flour seasoned to taste with
 salt and pepper
$1/4$ cup olive oil
$1/2$ cup (or to taste) sliced,
 toasted almonds
1 tablespoon finely chopped
 parsley
2 tablespoons fresh lemon
 juice
$1^{1}/4$ cups Chablis
2 tablespoons (or more, if
 desired) capers
3 drops Tabasco sauce
$1^{1}/4$ sticks butter
Toasted almond slices for
 garnish (optional)

Heat olive oil in skillet. Dredge fish in seasoned flour and shake off excess. Put fillets in heated oil and saute until golden brown on each side.

Remove fillets from skillet and set aside.

Discard any remaining olive oil in skillet. Deglaze pan with wine. Stir in almonds, parsley, lemon juice, capers and hot sauce.

Add butter. Stir until butter is melted and the sauce thickens.

Serve warm fish fillets topped with almond-caper sauce.

Garnish with additional toasted almond slices, if desired.

Makes 4 servings.

The hotel's restaurant is a favorite spot for theatergoers in downtown Orlando. Serve this apple dish with pork or chicken.

Omni International's Spiced Apples
Orlando

2 large Red Delicious apples
$\frac{1}{4}$ cup lemon juice
1 stick butter
4 teaspoons brown sugar
$\frac{1}{2}$ teaspoon cinnamon
$\frac{1}{8}$ cup sliced almonds
$\frac{1}{4}$ cup raisins

Preheat oven to 350F.

Wash and remove stems from apples; cut each in half and remove cores. Place fruit in small baking dish, cut side up.

Brush with lemon juice. Melt butter and pour $\frac{1}{4}$ cup over apples.

Mix together brown sugar, cinnamon, sliced almonds, raisins and remaining melted butter. Spread evenly over apples.

Bake until apples are tender and pan mixture is golden brown.

Makes 4 servings.

The Kapok Tree is no longer open, but in its heyday people would drive from all over Florida to dine at the Clearwater restaurant.

Kapok Tree's Corn Fritters
Clearwater

1 cup flour
1½ teaspoons baking powder
1 tablespoon sugar
1 teaspoon salt
1 egg
¼ cup milk
½ cup whole kernel canned
    corn
Fat for deep-frying
Confectioners' sugar

Sift flour, baking powder, sugar and salt together.

Add egg, milk and corn to dry ingredients.

In a deep-fryer, heat fat to 350F. Drop batter by the teaspoonful. Fry until golden brown on all sides.

Drain fritters on paper towels. Place on a serving platter and sprinkle with sugar.

Makes 16 servings.

The Park Bench is a charming restaurant overlooking Mount Dora's Donnelly Park. The quaint eatery is operated by Betty and Gary O'Neil. Betty bakes the pastries and Gary orchestrates the other culinary activity.

The Park Bench's Tomato Corn Salsa
Mount Dora

2 large or 3 medium tomatoes, diced
1 yellow or green bell pepper, diced
4 whole scallions, bulbs and greens, diced
2 cloves garlic, diced
1 cup fresh or frozen corn kernels, cooked
2 tablespoons chopped cilantro
2 tablespoons chopped parsley
1 tablespoon balsamic vinegar
Juice of 1 lime or lemon
4 tablespoons olive oil
Few drops hot sauce
Salt to taste
Cayenne or black pepper to taste

In large bowl, combine all ingredients.

Refrigerate at least 2 hours to chill thoroughly. Serve cold as topping for grilled, broiled or blackened fish.

Makes 6 condiment servings.

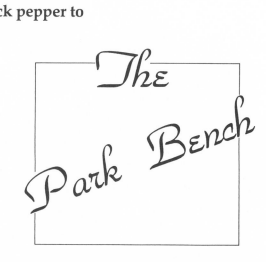

Serve these refried beans as a side dish to your favorite Mexican foods or as a dip for corn chips.

Paco's Refried Beans
Winter Park

1 (12-ounce) package dried
   pinto beans
1 large onion, chopped
Salt and pepper to taste
1 tablespoon garlic powder
¼ cup vegetable oil

Wash and pick over dried beans. Place in large kettle or Dutch oven, cover with water 3 to 4 times more than the volume of beans. Add remaining ingredients. Bring mixture to a boil, turn down heat and simmer until beans are soft and creamy, about 4 hours.

Put bean mixture in mixer bowl and beat until lightly mashed. Refrigerate overnight. When ready to serve, place beans in an oiled iron skillet and bake in 350F oven until bubbly and heated through.

Makes about 6 servings.

Caterer Fred Fenwick started serving this side dish years ago when he operated Dake's The Big Sandwich Place on South Orange Avenue. His catering clients can still sample this Louisiana specialty.

Fenwick Catering's Red Beans and Rice
Orlando

1 pound dried red kidney
   beans
2 quarts water
6 tablespoons bacon
   drippings, divided
4 cloves garlic, minced
1 large onion, chopped
2 green bell peppers, chopped
2 red bell peppers, chopped
1 whole stalk (6 to 8 ribs)
   celery, chopped
1 (16-ounce) can tomatoes,
   chopped (reserve juice)
1 to 1½ quarts water
½ teaspoon red pepper
   flakes
1 teaspoon dried thyme leaves
¼ pound diced ham
2 pounds hot smoked sausage,
   cut into ¼-inch slices
Salt and pepper to taste
Tabasco sauce to taste
   (optional)
Cooked rice

Wash and pick over dry beans. Combine with 2 quarts of water and soak overnight.

In a stockpot, melt 4 tablespoons bacon drippings. Add garlic and chopped vegetables and saute lightly. Add remaining water.

Drain beans and add to stockpot. Stir in pepper flakes and thyme leaves. Bring mixture to a soft boil. Reduce heat to simmer.

In a skillet, saute ham and sausage with remaining bacon drippings. When meat is lightly browned, add to stockpot. Stir mixture gently to make sure ingredients are well-mixed. Continue cooking for about 45 minutes, or until beans are tender but not mushy. Season with salt and pepper and, if desired, more red pepper flakes or Tabasco pepper sauce.

Serve in individual bowls with cooked rice.

Makes 8 to 10 servings.

A good Southern breakfast wouldn't be complete without grits. These cheese-drenched grits are delicious.

Pittypat's Porch's Grits Casserole
Atlanta

1 cup regular grits
3 cups boiling water
½ teaspoon salt
½ stick butter or margarine
4 eggs
1 cup milk
¼ cup shredded Cheddar
cheese

In a large Dutch oven, add salt to boiling water. Add grits and cook until thickened. Add the butter or margarine, beaten eggs, milk and cheese.

Preheat oven to 350F.

Grease a 2-quart casserole dish. Pour grits mixture into prepared dish and bake for about 30 minutes.

Makes 4 to 6 servings.

This side dish gets its flavor from a zesty mixture of vinegar, sugar and mustard powder. Serve it with broiled beef or pork.

Sleepy Hollow's Sweet-Sour Brussels Sprouts
Orlando

4 slices uncooked bacon, diced
2 (10-ounce) packages frozen
    brussels sprouts, thawed or
    equivalent amount fresh
    sprouts
1/4 cup diced onion
1/4 cup white vinegar
2 tablespoons sugar
1 teaspoon salt
1 teaspoon white pepper
1/4 teaspoon dry mustard
    powder

Fry bacon crisp. Drain the bacon on paper towels. Leave bacon drippings in skillet.

Add brussels sprouts and balance of ingredients (except bacon) to skillet. Stir well and cover skillet. Cook over medium-high heat, stirring occasionally, about 10 minutes.

Stir in bacon and serve warm. Makes 6 servings.

Here's a hearty side dish from Winter Park Memorial Hospital's kitchen! It's a favorite of the staff and patients.

Winter Park Memorial's Eggplant Casserole
Winter Park

2½ pounds eggplant
Salted water
3 eggs
1¼ cups (1 percent) low-fat milk
3 tablespoons margarine
2½ cups dry bread crumbs
½ cup chopped onions
1¼ cups margarine-coated bread crumbs
1¼ cups grated American cheese, divided

Peel eggplant and cut in 1-inch cubes. Boil in salted water for 6 to 8 minutes; drain.

Heat oven to 325F.

In a medium-size bowl, combine eggplant cubes, eggs, milk, margarine, dry bread crumbs and onions.

Pour into a greased baking pan. Top with margarine-coated bread crumbs. Sprinkle with grated cheese.

Bake for 20 to 30 minutes.

Makes 12 servings.

A bowlful of barbecue sauce is a welcome addition to any cookout. Slather it on grilled beef, chicken or fish.

Pioneer Hall's Barbecue Sauce
Fort Wilderness Resort, Lake Buena Vista

1 cup tomato puree
2 cups ketchup
1 cup cider vinegar
2 tablespoons soy sauce
1/3 cup sherry
1/2 cup vegetable oil
1 teaspoon Worcestershire
    sauce
2 teaspoons Liquid Smoke
2 teaspoons salt
2 teaspoons dry mustard
1 teaspoon bottled barbecue
    seasoning (available in the
    spice section of most
    supermarkets)
1/2 cup sugar
1 clove garlic, finely chopped
3 teaspoons cornstarch
1/3 cup water

Combine all ingredients except cornstarch and water in a large saucepan. Bring mixture to a boil.

Dissolve cornstarch in water and stir into sauce. Let cook until thickened; remove pan from heat and cool sauce.

Sauce can be used on chicken, beef or pork. Refrigerate unused sauce.

Makes 5 cups.

The restaurant's full name is a mouthful – Alfredo the Original Di Roma. This tomato concoction can be used on pasta or chicken.

Alfredo's Marinara Sauce
Italian Showcase, Epcot Center, Lake Buena Vista

½ cup vegetable oil
1 head fresh garlic, chopped
    (or more to taste)
⅔ cup chopped fresh parsley
4 ounces salted anchovies,
    chopped
6 (16-ounce) cans peeled
    tomatoes, chopped
Salt and pepper to taste

In a large Dutch oven or casserole dish, saute garlic in oil until it turns slightly brown. Add parsley and anchovies and cook for 1 minute. Add tomatoes, salt and pepper and simmer for 20 minutes.

Makes about 20 servings.

Chef Tony Pace's Dijon Sauce is basically a smooth hollandaise that gets a zesty kick from a splash of mustard. The degree of mustard pungency can be adjusted to suit the cook's preference.

Pebbles' Dijon Sauce
Lake Buena Vista, Longwood, Orlando, Winter Park

1 egg yolk
1 teaspoon water
4 ounces warm clarified butter
Juice of ½ lemon
Dash of cayenne pepper
Salt and white pepper to taste
Granulated garlic to taste
1 tablespoon white wine
Dijon mustard to taste

Whisk egg yolk with water until frothy. Gradually stir in warm clarified butter. Add lemon juice, salt, peppers and garlic.

Dissolve mustard in white wine until emulsified. Blend into sauce. Bring to room temperature to serve.

Makes 2 servings.

Serve this sauce over vegetables, seafood or chicken. To get more juice out of your lemon, microwave the uncut fruit on high (100 percent) power for 15 seconds before squeezing.

Pebbles' Lemon Dill Sauce
Lake Buena Vista, Longwood, Orlando, Winter Park

2 tablespoons unsalted butter
1 tablespoon neutral stock, such as chicken or veal
Juice of ½ lemon
1 tablespoon chopped fresh dill (chopped parsley may be substituted)

In a saute pan, brown butter until it begins to froth. Remove pan from heat. Stir in stock and lemon juice until emulsified. Add chopped dill and serve with seafood.

Makes 2 servings.

Lombardi's is located in the elegant Olympia Place office building, just a couple of blocks from Lake Ivanhoe.

Lombardi's Italian Roasted Potatoes
Orlando

1 cup vegetable oil
1 pound small Red Bliss
   potatoes, quartered
1 tablespoon diced pancetta
   (Italian bacon)
1 teaspoon chopped fresh
   rosemary
1 medium-size yellow onion,
   finely diced
Salt and pepper to taste

In a heavy roasting pan, brown potatoes in oil on high heat, stirring occasionally. Drain oil from pan and reserve.

Bake browned potatoes in a 375F oven for 15 minutes.

Put 2 tablespoons of reserved oil in a medium-size skillet. (Discard any remaining oil.) Heat oil and add pancetta. Saute until lightly brown. Stir in onions and caramelize. Add rosemary.

Remove potatoes from oven and toss with onion mixture. Season to taste with salt and pepper. Serve immediately.

Makes 4 servings.

Desserts

This popular dessert at Gary's Duck Inn is prepared for the restaurant from a Bailey's Original Irish Cream Liqueur recipe.

Gary's Bailey's White Chocolate Mousse Pie
Orlando

1 pound white chocolate
1 stick unsalted butter
4 egg yolks
8 egg whites
1 cup heavy cream
1/2 cup Bailey's Irish Cream
   Liqueur
Whipped cream for garnish
Shaved chocolate for garnish

Chocolate crust:
2 cups fine chocolate wafer
   crumbs
6 tablespoons melted unsalted
   butter

To make the chocolate crumb crust, mix 2 cups fine chocolate wafer crumbs with 6 tablespoons melted unsalted butter. Press onto bottom and sides of a buttered 10-inch pie pan. Crumb shell should be thin. Chill before filling with mousse.

Melt white chocolate in top of double boiler over barely simmering water, stirring until smooth. Melt butter (it should be warm, not hot) and combine with white chocolate in a mixing bowl until smooth. Beat egg yolks until thick and pale in color. Add egg yolks to chocolate mixture and whisk until smooth. Beat egg whites until soft peaks form and fold into chocolate mixture. Whip cream until soft peaks form and gently fold into mousse. Carefully stir in Bailey's. Pour into the chocolate crust and refrigerate until set, at least 2 hours. Garnish with whipped cream rosettes and chocolate shavings just before serving.

Makes 1 (10-inch) pie or 8 servings.

As owner-chef of Sweets Etcetera, Jim Alexander has been baking desserts for many of the area's better restaurants. The following pie is a perfect ending for a Thanksgiving Day feast.

Sweets Etcetera's Sweet Potato Pecan Pie
Orlando

1 (9-inch) deep-dish pie shell, unbaked
2$\frac{1}{2}$ cups firmly packed cooked sweet potatoes
$\frac{1}{4}$ cup firmly packed dark brown sugar
$\frac{1}{3}$ cup granulated sugar
1 egg
1 ounce heavy cream
$\frac{3}{4}$ teaspoon ground cinnamon
$\frac{3}{4}$ cup chopped pecans

Syrup:
1 egg
1 ounce molasses
$\frac{1}{4}$ cup corn syrup
$\frac{1}{3}$ cup granulated sugar
$\frac{1}{2}$ teaspoon vanilla
1 tablespoon melted margarine

Put sweet potatoes, brown sugar, $\frac{1}{3}$ cup granulated sugar, 1 egg, heavy cream and cinnamon in the work bowl of a mixer or food processor. Blend ingredients well.

Spread mixture in unbaked pie shell. Sprinkle with chopped pecans; set aside.

Preheat oven to 350F.

To make syrup, mix 1 egg, molasses, corn syrup, $\frac{1}{3}$ cup granulated sugar, vanilla and margarine. Pour syrup evenly over pecan pie topping.

Put pie in preheated oven and bake for 1 hour and 15 minutes.

Makes 6 to 8 servings.

SWEETS ETCETERA

This pie was created by Donna Douthitt. Chef Buster Silva says this dessert and the Banana Cream Pie are Lido's most requested menu items.

Lido's Chocolate Peanut Butter Pie
Orlando

Crust:
2 cups graham cracker crumbs
3 tablespoons sugar
2 teaspoons cinnamon
1 stick butter, melted

Filling:
1 package unflavored gelatin
1/3 cup cold water
2/3 cup sugar
3 tablespoons cornstarch
3 jumbo eggs, separated
2 1/2 cups milk
1 1/2 cups crunchy peanut butter
1 (8-ounce) container La Creme topping
1/2 cup Nestle's Toll House morsels
2 tablespoons water

Heat oven to 325F.

Combine all ingredients listed for crust and press into a 9 1/2 -inch deep-dish pie pan. Bake in the oven for 15 minutes. Remove crust from oven and set aside.

Dissolve unflavored gelatin in cold water and set aside.

In a double boiler, combine sugar, cornstarch, egg yolks and milk. Cook over boiling water, stirring constantly, until thickened. Remove from heat and add softened gelatin. Pour custard into a large bowl and add peanut butter. Combine thoroughly and set aside to cool mixture to room temperature.

Beat egg whites until stiff. Gently fold egg whites into custard. Fold in La Creme topping and refrigerate filling for 30 minutes.

Melt chocolate chips in water. Remove chocolate mixture from heat and let cool. Pour filling into crust. Drizzle with melted chocolate. Using a fork, make a swirl pattern in the pie.

Refrigerate pie at least 6 hours before serving.

Makes 12 servings.

This fabulous pie contains no whipped topping. It's a combination of whipping cream and creamy peanut butter custard.

Stouffer Orlando Resort's Peanut Butter Pie
Orlando

1 cup milk
1 envelope unflavored gelatin
³/₄ cup sugar, divided
¹/₄ teaspoon salt
4 eggs, separated
1 teaspoon vanilla
¹/₂ cup peanut butter
¹/₂ cup whipping cream,
   whipped
1 (9-inch) pie shell, baked
Chopped peanuts for garnish

Chocolate glaze:
6 ounces semisweet chocolate
   morsels
¹/₃ cup evaporated milk
1 cup powdered sugar
¹/₂ cup honey

Put milk in the top of double boiler and heat over simmering water. Soften gelatin in the milk. Add ¹/₄ cup sugar, salt and egg yolks and beat slightly just to blend. Cook, stirring constantly, until mixture thickens and coats a metal spoon. Remove pan from heat. Add vanilla and beat in peanut butter. Chill mixture until thickened but not firm.

Beat egg whites until foamy. Gradually add remaining sugar, beating until stiff but not dry. Fold meringue mixture into peanut butter mixture. Gently fold in whipped cream.

Pile filling lightly into pie shell. Chill pie until firm.

To make chocolate glaze, combine chocolate morsels and evaporated milk in a saucepan. Stir mixture over low heat until chocolate is melted. Remove from heat and stir in powdered sugar. Add honey and beat until smooth.

When pie is thoroughly chilled and firm, coat top with chocolate glaze. Sprinkle with chopped peanuts and serve.

Makes 8 servings.

This pie is not only lush, it is incredibly simple to prepare. The recipe was developed by Betty O'Neil who runs the charming Lake County restaurant with her husband Gary.

Park Bench's Butterscotch Pecan Pie
Mount Dora

1 (9-inch) unbaked deep-dish
   pie shell
1 cup sugar
1 cup light corn syrup
1/4 cup real maple syrup
1/2 stick butter
4 eggs, beaten
1 1/2 cups butterscotch morsels
2 cups pecan halves, or as
   desired
Ice cream or whipped cream
   (optional)

Preheat oven to 325F.

In saucepan, heat sugar, corn syrup, maple syrup and butter just until butter melts. Gently blend ingredients. Remove pan from heat and cool to room temperature. Stir in beaten eggs.

Line bottom of pie shell with butterscotch morsels. Pour filling into shell.

Arrange pecan halves on top and bake in preheated oven for 55 minutes. Cool pie. Serve cold or at room temperature. Top with ice cream or whipped cream if desired.

Makes 10 servings.

Recipe notes: The filling will fill a 9-inch deep dish pie shell almost to the rim. In the oven, place a pan under the pie shell to catch any drips or spills.

After 55 minutes, the center of the pie may not be firm. Turn off the heat and leave the pie in the oven until it is completely cool. It will firm up just fine.

If deep-dish pie shells are unavailable, use 2 regular-size shells.

Christine and Richard Annis operate Mount Dora's Windsor Rose Tea Room. Richard says the key to this recipe's success is beating the batter to an aerated froth and baking in an oven that's not too hot.

Windsor Rose's Victoria Sponge Cake
Mount Dora

1$\frac{1}{3}$ cups self-rising flour
$\frac{5}{8}$ cup sugar
3 medium eggs, beaten
1 tablespoon vanilla
1$\frac{1}{2}$ sticks butter, melted
Betty Crocker Sour Cream
   Frosting
Strawberry jam
Confectioners' sugar
6 large fresh strawberries
   with caps

Blend flour and sugar with an electric mixer. On medium speed, beat in eggs and vanilla. Stir in butter, beat to frothy consistency, about 3 or 4 minutes. Start on low speed and mix about 1 minute, circle sides of bowl with spatula to smooth down batter. Increase speed to high and beat another 1$\frac{1}{2}$ minutes.

Heat oven to 300F.

Butter an 8-inch round cake pan (or line with wax paper). Pour batter into prepared pan. Bake for about 40 to 45 minutes. When cake begins to crack, check for doneness. Gently press center of cake; if it quivers, return to oven about 5 minutes. Center should spring back when checked.

Cool for 20 minutes. Cake will pop out best if slightly warm. Cool cake and split in half crosswise. Spread sour cream frosting thickly on bottom layer. Cover frosting lightly with jam, leaving sour cream frosting on outer rim untouched. Add top layer. Dust with confectioners' sugar. Halve berries and arrange so that a berry is included on each slice.

Makes 8 to 10 servings.

Present this dessert in a chafing dish. It will make a spectacular presentation for brunch or dinner. Smaller portions of Marinated Bananas can be served over vanilla ice cream.

Mission Inn's Marinated Bananas
Howey-in-the-Hills

8 ounces light corn syrup
1 tablespoon cinnamon
1 tablespoon nutmeg
1 cup sugar
1 tablespoon lemon juice
2 tablespoons brandy
¼ cup water
6 well-ripened bananas, sliced
   lengthwise, then cut in
   2-inch lengths
Freshly whipped cream for
   garnish (optional)

Combine all ingredients except bananas and whipped cream in a saucepan, blend well. Bring mixture to a light boil. Remove from heat and cool to room temperature. Toss bananas into mixture.

Present in chafing dish or serve in individual glass bowls.

Garnish each with whipped cream, if desired.

Makes 6 servings.

MISSION INN
GOLF AND TENNIS RESORT

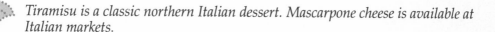

Tiramisu is a classic northern Italian dessert. Mascarpone cheese is available at Italian markets.

Caruso's Palace's Tiramisu-Gateau
Orlando

1 thin (10-inch) vanilla sponge cake layer (see note)
1 pound, 2 ounces mascarpone cheese (see note)
½ cup sugar
4 egg yolks (see note)
Pinch of salt
2 cups lightly sweetened, lightly whipped cream
5 (½-ounce) ladyfingers (see note)
¼ cup Amaretto liqueur or coffee brandy to mix with simple syrup
2 cups stiffly whipped cream, slightly sweetened
Cocoa powder for garnish

¾ cup simple syrup:
½ cup water
¼ pound white sugar

Place 10-inch vanilla sponge layer in a 10-inch springform pan. Wrap pan's exterior seams with aluminum foil to seal. Blend marscapone cheese, sugar, egg yolks and salt. Fold in 2 cups whipped cream. Place half of this mixture on sponge cake, spread evenly.

To make simple syrup, boil sugar and water over high heat until sugar dissolves. Blend with Amaretto. Put ladyfingers on mascarpone filling and moisten with simple syrup mixture. Cover with remaining mascarpone mix. Refrigerate for 4 to 5 hours.

Frost cake with stiffly whipped cream. Dust with cocoa powder.

Makes 8 servings.

Recipe notes: Mascarpone cheese is available in Italian markets and some specialty stores. Ladyfingers are fat finger-shaped cookies.

Locating a ready-made 10-inch vanilla sponge cake may be a challenge. Some bakeries will sell them as special-order items.

This traditional recipe uses uncooked egg yolks. Pasteurized egg substitutes may be used, if preferred.

CARUSO'S PALACE

Jim and Sheila Alexander are both graduates of the Culinary Institute of America in Hyde Park, N.Y. Their Sweets Etcetera bakery and Thornton Park Cafe are favorite stops for folks who frequent downtown Orlando.

Thornton Park Cafe's Mississippi Mud Cake
Orlando

2 cups water
3 tablespoons instant coffee
    granules
1 teaspoon salt
2 cups sugar
1 (6-ounce) package semisweet
    chocolate chips
1½ cups vegetable oil
1 teaspoon vanilla
1½ cups cocoa powder
1½ cups all-purpose flour
1 tablespoon baking soda
3 large eggs

Icing:
1 (6-ounce) package semisweet
    chocolate chips
5 ounces heavy whipping
    cream

Heat oven to 325F.

Put water, coffee, salt, sugar and chips in a microwave-safe bowl. Cover with plastic wrap and vent. Cook in the microwave on high (100 percent power) for 4 minutes. Remove bowl. Stir with a wire whisk to blend mixture well; set aside.

Combine oil and vanilla. Stir in melted chocolate. Mix chocolate mixture, oil and vanilla on low speed. Leaving mixer running, sift cocoa powder, flour and baking soda together. Spoon mixture into bowl. Resume mixing on low speed until ingredients are incorporated. With mixer at low speed, add 3 eggs and continue mixing to smooth out batter.

Coat a bundt pan with non-stick spray. Dust with cocoa powder. Pour batter into pan and bake for 1 hour or until cake tests done. Let cake rest in pan for 10 minutes. Invert pan onto plate and refrigerate to chill.

To make icing, put semisweet chips and heavy cream in a microwave-safe bowl. Cover with plastic wrap and vent. Microwave on high for 2 minutes. Stir to blend. Chill until it thickens to desired consistency. Swirl icing over cake.

Makes 16 servings.

The Gables in Mount Dora is a longtime favorite for leisurely lunches and fabulous dinners. The desserts are always top-rate.

The Gables' Chocolate Pecan Pie
Mount Dora

⅓ pound butter or margarine
6 ounces Hershey's dry cocoa
1 cup granulated sugar
¼ cup oil
1⅓ cups white Karo syrup
5 whole eggs, lightly beaten
2 teaspoons vanilla
2 cups chopped pecans
Whipped cream or ice cream
   (optional)
1 (10-inch) pie shell

Preheat oven to 350F.

In a saucepan, melt butter. Add dry cocoa, sugar and oil and stir until well-blended.

Add syrup, eggs, vanilla and pecans, mixing well.

Pour into pie shell and bake in oven for 50 minutes to 1 hour.

Cool pie and refrigerate overnight.

Serve chilled or slightly warm topped with vanilla ice cream or whipped cream.

Makes 8 servings.

This is one of the easiest key lime pie recipes around. Simply mix, cook briefly and refrigerate for a refreshing taste treat.

Gary's Duck Inn's Key Lime Pie
Orlando

6 ounces fresh or frozen lime juice (not in concentrate form)

28 ounces sweetened condensed milk (not evaporated)

1 (9-inch) graham cracker or chocolate-cookie crumb crust

Bring lime juice to a boil. Just as it begins to boil, remove from heat and refrigerate about 15 minutes. Stir lime juice into condensed milk and pour into pie shell. Place in refrigerator. If graham cracker crust is used, serve topped with fresh whipped cream and garnish with lime slice. If chocolate crust is used, scatter chocolate sprinkles on top of pie.

Makes 6 to 8 servings.

The dessert cart is always a welcome sight at the Citrus Club. This pie is made in the original Key West tradition.

Citrus Club's Key Lime Pie
Orlando

1 (9-inch) graham cracker
    crumb crust
2 (14-ounce) cans Eagle Brand
    condensed (not evaporated)
    milk
4 egg yolks, beaten
¾ cup lime juice
1 tablespoon grated lime peel
1 pint heavy cream, whipped
Mint leaves
8 lime slices

Mix condensed milk with egg yolks, lime juice and lime peel. Pour into pie crust. Bake 5 minutes in 300F oven. Refrigerate for 1 hour. Cover with whipped cream; garnish with lime slices and mint leaves.

Makes 6 to 8 servings.

CITRUS CLUB

Charlie's is recognized for its specialty cakes and American and European pastries. Master baker Charlie Hawks established the bakery in 1972. His son, Gary, carries on the tradition as manager.

Charlie's Gourmet Pastries' Peanut Butter Pie
Orlando

2 cups milk
4 egg yolks
2 tablespoons sugar
1 cup creamy peanut butter
1 (9-inch) baked pie crust
Whipped cream and chopped
   peanuts for garnish

Put milk in a saucepan on low heat until milk is very hot, but do not allow it to boil.

Beat yolks and sugar in a bowl, add hot milk slowly. Place in a double boiler and cook, stirring continuously, until mixture has thickened. Remove from heat, add peanut butter and mix until smooth and blended. Pour into baked 9-inch pastry shell. Chill for several hours or overnight before serving.

To serve, top portions with whipped cream and chopped peanuts.

Makes 6 to 8 servings.

This sinful treat is similar to Pebbles' White Chocolate Bread Pudding. Brioche is a French yeast bread available by special order at full-service bakeries.

Pebbles' Chocolate Bread Pudding
Lake Buena Vista, Longwood, Orlando, Winter Park

1½ pounds brioche
½ pound butter, melted
1 cup milk
3 cups heavy cream
10 egg yolks, beaten
1½ cups sugar
1 pound bittersweet chocolate
½ tablespoon vanilla
Vanilla Brandy Sauce (recipe
   follows)

Remove crusts from brioche. Cut into cubes and dip in butter. Put on baking sheet and toast in oven. Arrange bread in a buttered 2- to 2¹/₂-inch deep pan (12 or 13 inches square). Bring milk and cream to a boil; remove from heat. Add a little of the hot mixture to yolks to bring up the temperature. Whisk yolks and sugar into milk mixture. Melt chocolate. Stir chocolate into custard. Stir in vanilla. Pour over bread. Work custard into bread. Let stand for 1 hour. Heat oven to 325F. Put pan in larger pan with hot water coming halfway up sides to make a water bath. Bake for 1 hour. Serve with sauce.

Makes 12 servings.

Vanilla Brandy Sauce

¼ cup white chocolate
¼ cup heavy cream, whipped
3 tablespoons brandy

Melt white chocolate in double boiler. Remove from heat source. Let cool at room temperature. Using a wooden spoon, gently fold in whipped cream. Stir in brandy or liqueur of choice. Refrigerate. Serve cold over bread pudding.

Makes about ¹/₂ cup.

This amazing dessert gets a flavor kick from a coffee liqueur. It was developed by Sweets Etcetera's owner and master baker Jim Alexander.

Sweets Etcetera's Chocolate Kahlua Cheesecake
Orlando

2 pounds cream cheese
1/4 cup firmly packed dark
   brown sugar
1 1/4 cups sugar
1/4 cup all-purpose flour
1 1/2 teaspoons instant coffee,
   divided use
6 ounces Kahlua, divided use
5 eggs
7 ounces semisweet chocolate
   chips

Put cream cheese, dark brown sugar, white sugar, flour, 1/2 teaspoon of the instant coffee and 3 ounces of the Kahlua in a mixer bowl. Using a flat beater, mix ingredients until smooth. Then, with machine running, add eggs one at a time and continue beating until all ingredients are incorporated and smooth.

Melt chocolate chips with remaining instant coffee and Kahlua in the microwave oven on high (100 percent) power for 1 1/2 minutes. Remove from microwave oven and whisk by hand until smooth. Add about 2 cups of the cream cheese batter to the chocolate mixture and mix thoroughly by hand.

Heat oven to 250F.

Pour this mixture on top of the remaining cream cheese mixture and swirl a couple of times with a rubber spatula. Pour resulting batter into a buttered 9-inch springform pan and smooth the surface with the rubber spatula. Bake in oven for 1 hour and 45 minutes. When done, chill in refrigerator. Remove from springform pan and serve.

Makes 10 servings.

A nutty candy bar inspired this sinful dessert. It can be found on the menu at Florida Bay restaurants and Thornton Park Cafe.

Sweets Etcetera's Snickers Cheesecake
Orlando

1 (9-inch) unbaked pie shell
1½ pounds cream cheese, cut into cubes
1¼ cups sugar
1 teaspoon vanilla
3 eggs, divided
6 regular size Snickers bars
2 ounces caramels
1 tablespoon whipping cream
2 ounces semisweet chocolate morsels
3 tablespoons whipping cream
Chopped peanuts for garnish

Heat oven to 350F.

Using a 9-inch pie shell, remove fluted rim (reserve for another use) and place pie shell in bottom of 9-inch springform pan. Bake in oven until golden brown. When pan has cooled, grease the sides and set aside.

Mix cream cheese, sugar, vanilla and 1 egg until smooth. Scrape down sides of bowl with spatula and add 2 remaining eggs. Mix until blended.

Lower oven temperature to 275F.

Cut each candy bar lengthwise once, then cut crosswise into 14 to 16 pieces. Fold candy into cream cheese batter. Pour batter into crust. Bake for 2 hours. Cool completely in refrigerator. Remove from pan and put on a serving plate.

Melt caramels with 1 tablespoon whipping cream in microwave oven. Remove from microwave and blend with whisk. Spread caramel on top of cheesecake to within 1 inch of edge.

Melt semisweet chocolate morsels with 3 tablespoons whipping cream in microwave oven. Blend with whisk. Spread on top of caramel coating to within ½-inch of the edge. Sprinkle top of cheesecake with chopped peanuts.

Makes 12 servings.

This presentation was developed by chef Philippe M. Gehin. His recipe is divided into three steps: chocolate mousse, chocolate squares, and a delicate cream sauce.

Park Plaza Gardens' Ebony and Ivory
Winter Park

Chocolate mousse:
5 tablespoons unsalted butter
$1^1/_2$ ounces imported
    semisweet chocolate
$^1/_2$ cup unsweetened Dutch
    process cocoa
2 egg yolks
$^1/_4$ cup sugar
2 tablespoons strong brewed
    coffee
2 tablespoons water
$^1/_2$ cup heavy cream, whipped
    until firm

Chocolate squares:
$2^1/_2$ ounces semisweet
    chocolate, 1 part sweetened,
    1 part unsweetened

Sauce:
$^1/_2$ cup cream
2 egg yolks
$^1/_2$ pound white chocolate
2 ounces sugar
2 tablespoons Cream of Cocoa
    liqueur
Mint leaves for garnish
    (optional)
Fresh raspberries for garnish
    (optional)
Whipped cream for garnish
    (optional)

Combine butter, $1^1/_2$ ounces chocolate and cocoa. Heat until melted. Beat yolks and sugar until pale and thick. Beat in coffee and water. Beat in chocolate mixture. With mixer on high, beat in whipped cream. Refrigerate for 2 hours.

Melt $2^1/_2$ ounces of chocolate. Let cool slightly. Put a sheet of parchment paper on a cookie sheet and weight down ends of paper. Draw an 8-by-10-inch rectangle. Spread chocolate mixture inside outline. Set aside to harden; do not refrigerate. When nearly firm, use a knife to score 12 rectangles. Let harden completely.

Bring $^1/_2$ cup of cream to a boil. Melt $^1/_2$ pound of white chocolate into the cream. Let mixture cool a bit. Whip 2 yolks and 2 ounces of sugar and fold the mixture into cream. The cream should not be boiling when you add the eggs. Stir in the liqueur. Spoon sauce onto 6 serving plates. Peel paper from chocolate. Put a rectangle in middle of each sauce pool. Add a dollop of chocolate mousse in center. Top each with another rectangle. Garnish with mint, berries and whipped cream.

Makes 6 servings.

The Dubsdread Restaurant and Lounge is located at 549 W. Par Ave. in the College Park section of Orlando. The eatery, which now features patio dining with fairway views, serves lunch and dinner daily.

Dubsdread's Apple Fritters
Orlando

6 Granny Smith apples
2 cups apple juice
$1/2$ cup sugar
1 teaspoon cinnamon
$1/4$ teaspoon nutmeg
1 ounce brandy
$1/4$ cup cornstarch dissolved in
  water
6 (5 $1/2$-by-5$1/2$-inch) puff
  pastry sheets (available in
  the frozen food sections of
  most supermarkets; follow
  package directions for
  thawing)
Cinnamon-flavored ice cream
Caramel sauce
Whipped cream (optional)

Peel and core apples and slice as for pie.

In a saucepan, bring apple juice, sugar, spices and brandy to a boil. Remove from heat and place apple slices in hot liquid. Let stand for 1 hour to cool.

Remove apples and set aside. Return liquid to a boil and cook until volume is reduced by one-third. Thicken with cornstarch dissolved in water. Set mixture aside.

Preheat oven to 375F.

Arrange puff pastry squares on a baking sheet.

Place apple slices in pinwheel fashion on top of each. Brush with reserved liquid to glaze.

Bake in oven for 8 to 10 minutes or until golden brown. Lightly glaze with more apple syrup.

Top with cinnamon ice cream, spoon on caramel sauce. If desired, add a pool of remaining apple syrup to each plate. Top with whipped cream and serve warm.

Makes 6 servings.

Orient IV host-owner Fred Sie serves these cookies at the conclusion of dinner. The restaurant is located at 120 International Parkway in Central Florida's upscale Heathrow area.

Orient IV's Almond Cookies
Lake Mary

4 cups all-purpose flour
2 cups sugar
1 teaspoon baking soda
1 pound Crisco shortening,
    softened, but not melted
3 medium eggs, divided
2 teaspoons almond extract
1 teaspoon yellow food color

Heat oven to 375F.

Combine flour, sugar and baking soda. Make a well in mixture and add Crisco, 2 eggs, almond extract and food coloring to the center of dry mix. Knead lightly with hands until mixture is a solid ball. Roll out on a flat surface to a 1-inch thick sheet. Cut sheet into $1^1/2$-inch squares (cookie sheet will look like a grid).

Line a flat baking pan with parchment or baking paper. Place cookie squares on pan, leaving about 2 inches between squares. Flatten each square with your hand to a $1/2$-inch thickness. (This will give the cookies a rounded shape.) Beat the remaining egg and brush liberally on each cookie (this is very important).

Bake for 5 minutes, rotate pan, and bake another 5 minutes. Turn oven off and rotate pan once more. Let cookies sit in cooling oven for another 4 to 5 minutes. (Oven temperatures vary and baking time must be adjusted accordingly.)

Remove cookies from oven and let cool thoroughly, about 10 minutes.

Sea World's Florida Festival closed in 1986 but Al E. Gator's restaurant continued to operate in the theme park until 1992. The eatery has been redesigned and is now called Bimini Bay.

Al E. Gator's Mango Muffins
Sea World, Orlando

2 cups flour
1/2 teaspoon salt
2 teaspoons baking powder
2 teaspoons cinnamon
3/4 cup oil
1 1/4 cups sugar
1 teaspoon vanilla extract
3 eggs
1/4 cup chopped walnuts
1/2 cup shredded coconut
1 package frozen shredded mangoes or 3 cups fresh diced mangoes

Sift flour, salt, baking powder and cinnamon together.

In a large bowl, combine sifted dry ingredients with remaining ingredients.

Preheat oven to 325F.

Grease muffin tins. Fill tins about two-thirds full with batter and let bake for 20 minutes.

Bake for 30 to 40 minutes.

Makes 12 muffins.

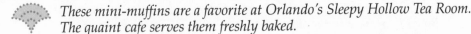

These mini-muffins are a favorite at Orlando's Sleepy Hollow Tea Room. The quaint cafe serves them freshly baked.

Sleepy Hollow's Orange Blossom Muffins
Orlando

1 box Duncan Hines white
   cake mix with pudding
3 eggs
$\frac{1}{4}$ cup vegetable oil
$\frac{1}{3}$ cup water
2 (5$\frac{1}{2}$-ounce) packages sugared
   orange slice candy, minced
   finely
1 (11-ounce) can mandarin
   oranges, drained and
   chopped
2 drops yellow food color
2 drops red food color

Preheat oven to 350F.

In large bowl mix all ingredients into white cake mix with pudding. Coat mini-muffin tins with nonstick cooking spray. Fill cups two-thirds full and bake for 15 minutes.

Makes 48 small muffins.

Recipe notes: Pillsbury cake mix can be substituted for the Duncan Hines mix.

The orange candy can be sticky when sliced. Don't be overly concerned about the sticking, it will separate when stirred into the batter.

The yield given above is for batter baked in muffin tins that measure 1$\frac{1}{2}$ inches across the bottom and 2$\frac{1}{4}$ inches across the top. Muffin tins that measure 1 inch across the bottom and 2 inches across the top will produce about 84 muffins.

This dessert was first introduced to Central Florida diners at Jordan's Grove in Maitland. It's another fabulous dessert from chef Jim Alexander.

Sweets Etcetera's Raspberry Cheesecake
Orlando

Crust:
1 cup blanched, sliced
    almonds
1 cup sugar
1 teaspoon baking soda
1 tablespoon lemon peel
3 cups flour
2 sticks butter or margarine,
    cut up
4 egg whites
Juice of 1 lemon

Raspberry jam:
$1^{1}/_{2}$ cups sugar
1 pound fresh or frozen
    unsweetened raspberries

Cheesecake filling:
10 ounces cream cheese,
    softened
$^{1}/_{2}$ cup sugar
3 tablespoons flour
$^{3}/_{4}$ cup reserved raspberry jam
    mixture
5 large eggs
1 egg white

Using a food processor fitted with a metal blade, process almonds, sugar, baking soda and lemon peel until the nuts are fine. Add 3 cups of flour and 2 sticks of butter. Process until mixture is crumbly. With machine running, add 4 egg whites and the lemon juice. Process mixture until smooth. Heat oven to 375F.

Pat out 1 cup of dough on bottom of a 9-inch springform pan. Bake until golden; set aside. (This makes enough dough for 5 crusts. The balance can be frozen for later use.)

Simmer $1^{1}/_{2}$ cups sugar and 1 pound of unsweetened raspberries until 1 cup of jam remains; set aside.

Blend cream cheese, $^{1}/_{2}$ cup sugar, 3 tablespoons of flour and $^{3}/_{4}$ cup of the reserved jam mixture until smooth and no lumps remain. Stop machine, scrape down sides of bowl, making a canal around outside. Into the canal put 5 eggs, 1 egg white and remainder of the jam mixture. Mix until blended. Lower oven to 250F. Pour cream cheese mixture over crust in greased 9-inch pan. Bake for about 3 hours, or until done (when pan is tapped on the side, contents move as one and there is no wave motion).

Makes 12 servings.

This is a grand dessert for a grand event and can be prepared well in advance of party time. The recipe will yield 12 servings.

Frozen Souffle Grand Marnier
Stouffer Orlando Resort

2½ cups sugar
½ cup water
13 egg yolks
1 quart heavy cream
1 cup Grand Marnier liqueur
4 ounces sliced almonds

Line inside of a 12- to 14-cup mold with grease-proof parchment or wax paper; leave about an inch showing above the mold to give frozen souffle the traditional appearance of a hot souffle.

In a small saucepan, cook sugar and water together until it forms small, firm balls when dropped from metal spoon into water or until temperature reaches 280F on a candy thermometer.

Add cooked sugar-water mixture gently to the egg yolks and whip until mixture is completely cooled.

In a mixer bowl, blend heavy cream with Grand Marnier and whip until soft peaks form. By hand, delicately blend whipped cream with egg yolk mixture.

Immediately fold this mixture into molds. With a spatula, smooth mixture to the edges of the paper. Freeze at least 3 hours. Sprinkle with sliced almonds.

The souffle may be served from mold. Remove paper from individual portions.

Makes 12 servings.

This is one of chef Tony Pace's signature desserts. It makes a festive presentation served in clear glass bowls and garnished with chopped nuts.

Pebbles' Gold Brick Chocolate Sundae
Lake Buena Vista, Longwood, Orlando, Winter Park

½ cup pure coconut oil
8 ounces bittersweet chocolate
½ cup confectioners' sugar
½ cup unsweetened cocoa
   powder
1 tablespoon unsalted butter
1 tablespoon brown sugar
⅓ cup Grand Marnier liqueur
4 to 6 fresh strawberries,
   halved
2 scoops premium vanilla ice
   cream
Chopped hazelnuts or
   pistachios for garnish
   (optional)

Heat oil to 200F.

In a food processor fitted with a metal blade, pulse chocolate with sugar and cocoa to coarsely chop, about 6 times. Process at a higher speed until mixture is as fine as sugar. With the machine running, pour hot oil through the feed tube and process until smooth. Set mixture aside, but keep warm.

In a saucepan over low heat, melt butter and brown sugar to caramelize. Carefully flame with liqueur and stir in berries.

Pour warm syrup in the bottom of 2 glass bowls or sundae dishes. Top each with a scoop of ice cream. Top with the hot bittersweet chocolate. Final topping will harden on the ice cream in a matter of seconds.

Garnish with chopped nuts if desired.

Makes 2 servings.

Recipe notes: Gold Brick brand chocolate topping, which is available near the ice cream in most supermarkets, may be substituted for the bittersweet chocolate topping.

Refrigerate or freeze unused bittersweet topping for another use.

Harvey's Bistro is the newest member of the Davgar family of restaurants, which includes Miami Subs, Florida Bay and Pebbles.

Harvey's Bistro's Chocolate-Raspberry Mousse
Orlando

5 (1-ounce) squares good-quality semisweet chocolate, such as Baker's and Lindt

¼ cup melted butter

2 egg yolks

1 tablespoon Myers's Dark Rum

2 egg whites

2 tablespoons sugar

½ cup heavy cream

½ container fresh raspberries

White chocolate shell purchased from a candy specialty store (optional)

Melt chocolate in the top of a double boiler. Whisk in melted butter. Remove mixture from heat and whisk in rum and egg yolks. Refrigerate mixture for 2 hours before serving.

In a bowl, beat egg whites until soft peaks form. Fold egg whites into chocolate mixture.

In another bowl, whip heavy cream and sugar until very soft peaks form.

Crush raspberries and gently blend with whipped cream. Refrigerate mixture for 2 hours before serving.

To serve, pipe or spoon into chilled dessert glasses or into a white chocolate shell.

Makes 4 servings.

Quinn's is a beachside restaurant at the Marco Island Resort. Chef Yves Favier developed the recipe for this creamy pie.

Quinn's Peanut Butter Pie
Marco Island

1 cup confectioners' sugar
1 cup cream cheese
1½ cups smooth peanut
   butter
½ cup heavy cream
1 cup sweetened whipped
   cream or whipped topping
Chocolate curls and crushed
   peanuts for garnish

Pie crust:
12 Oreo cookies, crushed
1½ tablespoons melted
   butter or margarine

To make pie crust, mix crushed Oreo cookies and melted butter or margarine. Press mixture into a 9-inch pie pan. Bake in a 350F oven for 5 minutes. Allow to cool before filling.

Blend confectioners' sugar and cream cheese until smooth. Add peanut butter and stir. Slowly mix in heavy cream. Fold in whipped cream, reserving some for garnish.

Pour into cooled pie shell and chill until set. Mound extra whipped cream on top. Garnish with chocolate curls and crushed peanuts. Chill pie until ready to serve.

Makes 8 servings.

Glossary

Adjust: When a recipe says to "adjust the seasonings," taste the dish at this stage of preparation. Add salt, spices or herbs, if needed, to balance the flavors.

Al dente: An Italian term for cooking pasta that translates "to the tooth." It means the pasta should be soft but have a firmness and bite.

Anisette: A clear, very sweet liqueur made from anise seed and tasting of licorice.

Arrowroot: A starchy thickener. Unlike cornstarch, it doesn't impart a chalky taste when undercooked.

Asiago: A semifirm Italian cheese with a rich, nutty flavor. It's made from whole or part-skim cow's milk. The yellow interior has many little holes.

Balsamic vinegar: A type of slightly sweet, smooth-tasting Italian wine vinegar that has been aged in oak barrels. It is not sour like American vinegar and be used alone on salads or cooked vegetables.

Bamboo shoots: The ivory colored shoot of an edible bamboo plant.

Basmati rice: This rice has a perfumy, nutlike flavor and aroma because the grain is aged to decrease its moisture content.

Bechamel: A basic French white sauce made by stirring milk into a butter-flour roux.

Bouquet garni: Herbs tied together in cheesecloth and used to flavor soups, stews or broths. The bouquet garni is removed before serving.

Brioche: A type of delicate French yeast roll made with butter and eggs.

Bruschetta: A classic warm Italian garlic toast that is drizzled with extra-virgin olive oil.

Butterfly: To split meat down the center, but not completely through. Called for most often in pork and shrimp dishes.

Cannelloni: Large pasta tubes that are boiled, then stuffed and baked in a sauce.

Carbonara: An Italian term describing pasta that is served with a sauce made of cream, eggs, Parmesan cheese and bacon.

Chanterelle: A trumpet-shaped wild mushroom that has a delicate, nutty taste.

Chickpea: Buff-colored legumes that have a firm texture and mild flavor. They are also called garbanzo beans and ceci.

Chutney: A spicy condiment that contains fruit, vinegar, sugar and spices. Chutney can be spread on bread or served with cheese.

Clarified butter: Also called drawn butter, this type has been cleared of all dairy solids.

Coddle: A cooking method used most often with eggs. There is cookware designed for coddling. However, the process can be accomplished by placing the food in a container that is covered, set in a larger pan of simmering water and placed either on the stove or in the oven on very low heat.

Consomme: A clarified meat or fish broth. Can be served hot or cold.

Cornstarch: A powdery flour from corn kernels. It is used to thicken puddings, sauces and soups. Because it has a tendency to clump, cornstarch is often mixed with a bit of cold water before adding to a hot liquid.

Couscous: This granular semolina is often sold precooked in supermarkets. Look for it near the rice.

Cream: To blend an ingredient with another to a smooth consistency.

Creme anglaise: A French term for a rich custard sauce. It is used in recipes or served alone over cake or fruit.

Deglaze: Heating a small amount of liquid (wine, water or juice) in a pan that has been used for cooking.

Demiglace: A rich brown sauce that is used as a base for many other sauces. It is available in some specialty food stores.

Dijon mustard: A prepared mustard flavored with white wine that originated in Dijon, France.

Egg wash: Egg yolk or white mixed with water or milk. It is brushed over baked foods before baking to give the foods color and gloss.

Fennel: A plant with green, celerylike stems and bright feathery foliage. It has a sweet licorice flavor. The broad, bulbous base can be braised, sauteed or added to soups. The feathery greenery can be snipped and used to add flavor or as a garnish.

Fold: A method of combining delicate ingredients, such as egg whites or whipped cream, with thicker ingredients. It is accomplished by using a spatula or spoon in a circular motion, cutting through the mixture, scraping along the bottom of the bowl and bringing some of the mixture back up to the top.

Fontina: A creamy semifirm cheese made from cow's milk. It has a mild, nutty flavor.

Grenadine: A ruby red pomegranate-flavored syrup used to color and flavor drinks and desserts.

Havarti: A semisoft, pale yellow cheese with a mild taste.

Lily buds: Also called tiger lily buds and golden needles, these dried buds of the tiger lily are 2 to 3 inches long and have a delicate, musky-sweet flavor. They are available in Asian markets.

Mace: Mace is the ground red membrane that covers the nutmeg seed.

Maggi Seasoning: A commercial browning liquid available at most supermarkets and health food stores.

Mascarpone: A buttery rich cream made from cow's milk. It's ivory colored and has a delicate texture. Shop for it in Italian markets and gourmet stores.

Morel: The spongy honeycombed, cone-shaped capped morel mushroom has a smoky, nutty flavor. Shop for fresh morels in specialty produce stores. Canned morels are often stocked in gourmet stores.

Mornay: A bechamel sauce to which cheese has been added. Mornay sauce is served with eggs, shellfish, vegetables and chicken.

MSG: An abbreviation for monosodium glutamate, a white crystalline powder that is used as a flavor enhancer. It has no pronounced flavor of its own.

Old Bay: A commercial seafood boil mixture sold in supermarkets.

Papillote: "En papillote" refers to food baked inside a wrapping of oiled parchment paper.

Parmigiano-Reggiano: Italy's pre-eminent Parmesan cheese. It has a granular texture that melts in the mouth. Parmigiano-Reggianos are often aged 2 years and come from Bologna, Mantua, Modena or Parma, Italy. It is available in Italian markets, specialty stores and some supermarkets.

Penne: Large tubes of pasta cut on the diagonal.

Pesto: An uncooked blend of fresh basil, garlic, pine nuts, Parmesan cheese and olive oil.

Prosciutto: Italian ham that is seasoned, salt-cured and air-dried. It is available in gourmet and specialty stores.

Ramekin: A single-serving baking dish that looks like a miniature souffle dish.

Reduce: To decrease the volume of a liquid by rapid boiling in an uncovered pan. As the volume is reduced, the flavors intensify and the consistency thickens.

Remoulade: A classic French sauce made from mayonnaise, mustard, capers, chopped gherkins, herbs and anchovies.

Render: To melt animal fat over low heat.

Roux: A blend of oil (or butter) and flour used to thicken sauces, gravies or soups.

Saltimbocca: Refers to a Roman specialty made of sliced veal sprinkled with sage and topped with a thin slice of prosciutto. This dish is sauteed in butter and braised in white wine. Sometimes the meat layers are rolled and secured with picks before cooking.

Sesame oil: A sesame seed oil that is made in light and dark varieties. It can be found in Asian markets, gourmet stores and supermarkets.

Spike: A commercial seasoning mixture available in health food stores and some supermarkets.

Stock: Strained liquid from cooking vegetables, meat, fish or shellfish in seasoned water. A brown stock is made by browning bones, vegetables and other ingredients before they are cooked.

Tofu: Also known as soy bean curd, tofu comes in a firm or soft texture. It is available in Asian markets, health food stores and some supermarkets.

Truffle: An extremely pungent fungus that has been prized by gourmets for centuries. Truffles are available in specialty shops and gourmet stores.

Veloute: A stock-based white sauce.

Water bath: The French call this cooking technique bain-marie. It involves placing a container (casserole dish, bowl, pan, etc.) in a large shallow pan of warm water during the cooking process. The bath surrounds the food with gentle heat. Water baths are used to cook delicate foods like souffle, custards and mousses.

Wood ear mushrooms: Also known as cloud ear, tree ear or silver ear, these mushrooms have a slightly crunchy texture and delicate taste. Available in Asian markets and some supermarkets.

Index

A

D

F

Fish

W

Recipe Notes

Recipe Notes

Recipe Notes

Recipe Notes

Enjoy More Sensational Tastes From Florida

Fresh from the Sunshine State comes the flavors and tastes that you'll love to share with friends and family. These cookbooks make great gifts or additions to your home cooking library.

A Taste of Florida

The first collection of the best recipes from Dorothy Chapman's reader request-based "Thought You'd Never Ask" column in *The Orlando Sentinel*, this cookbook lets you enjoy eating out without leaving the comfort of your home. Included are signature recipes from Central Florida's finest restaurants including some at Walt Disney World and Epcot Center.

Hardback with concealed wire binding, 224 pages, $18.95

The Florida Cookbook

Award-winning food writer Charlotte Balcomb Lane provides a healthy twist to old Southern favorites as well as Caribbean, Cajun and other ethnic dishes. *The Florida Cookbook* covers everything from appetizers to desserts and includes a chapter on menu planning.

Hardback with concealed wire binding, 224 pages, $18.95

Fish in a Flash

With more than 200 recipes, most of which can be prepared in 40 minutes or less, *Fish in a Flash,* by Charlotte Balcomb Lane is the perfect cookbook for those seeking to balance a healthy diet and an active schedule. And you don't have to live in Florida to enjoy fish, as the recipes use cuts and types of fish that are easy to find in grocery stores and fish markets.

Hardback with concealed wire binding, 224 pages, $18.95

Ordering Information

All cookbooks are available direct from Tribune Publishing.
Send check or money order for $18.95 per book plus shipping charges (see below) to:
Tribune Publishing, P.O. Box 1100, Orlando, Florida 32802

To order by phone, call
1/800/788-1225
Monday-Friday, 8 a.m. - 5 p.m., EST.

Shipping Charges
Shipping charge for one book is $3, for two books $4, and for three or more books $5.

Money Back Guarantee
If you are not completely satisfied with any of our books, simply return it and your money will be promptly and cheerfully refunded.